Ultimate Unofficial CSI Las Vegas Season One Guide: Crime Scene Investigation Las Vegas Season 1 Unofficial Guide

By: Kristina Benson

Ultimate Unofficial CSI Las Vegas Season One Guide: Crime Scene Investigation Las Vegas Season 1 Unofficial Guide

ISBN: 978-1-60332-025-2

Edited By: Brooke Winger

Table of Contents

Episode Guide

Pilot

This is the first episode of the first season of CSI Las Vegas.

Synopsis

The setting is Las Vegas, at night. We see bullets loaded into a gun, and the voiceover of a man making the declaration that his name is Royce Harmon and he is going to kill himself. A single shot is fired, and the black and whites arrive on the street, sirens screeching, bringing with them Captain Jim Brass and Gil Grissom.

Inside, Harmon's body is lying in a bathtub, his hand still stiffly clinging to the gun, wrapped in a sleeping bag. He has been here, dead in the bathtub, for seven days, and left a recorded suicide note. Brass and Grissom then play the tape for Royce Harmon's mother and sister, and immediately, the mother insists that this is not the voice of her son.

Back at the Crime Lab, Holly Gribbs reports to her first shift on the job, and meets Grissom, who then takes a pint of her blood. Also on their shifts are CSI's Warrick Brown and Nick Stokes. Warrick, a typical Las Vegas resident with a penchant for gambling, initiates a bet with Nick on which one of them will solve their 100th case by shift's end, thereby earning a Level 3 promotion. Another member of the team, Catherine Willows, arrives just as Jim Brass is delegating their caseloads for the evening, and assigning work.

Nick is assigned to investigate the case of a prostitute ripping off an incapacitated customer, an event called a trick roll in the crime solving industry. Catherine and Warrick are sent to investigate a home invasion involving a firearm. By the time they arrive, however, their home invasion has turned into a homicide. They step over the corpse lying across the front door. The man of the house tells them that after he threw the guy out for being an unwelcome houseguest, the victim kicked the door in, lunged menacingly, and the husband then shot the man. Upon close examination of the body, Catherine notes that the victim's left shoe is tied differently than the right, and the husband has got a cut on his left toe. These details, as well as others, make her and her partner skeptical about the husband's self defense claim.

Meanwhile the Medical Examiner tells Grissom and Holly that Harmon's death was not a suicide, and that he was the victim of foul play. Holly then excuses herself to be sick, seeking solitude in an adjoining room filled with dead bodies. The door closes and she hears the lock click behind her. to an adjoining room and the door locks behind her, leaving her alone with some dead bodies. She rapidly goes into hysterics until Grissom unlocks the door, and then drops her off at a local convenience store to process a routine robbery.

Nick, meanwhile, finds his rolled trick, John Laverty, dazed, groggy, and embarrassed in his hotel room. The call girl has liberated him of his wallet and wedding ring. Laverty doesn't think his drink was drugged, and when Nick takes a swab, nothing comes up.

Warrick, still doubting the homeowner's tale of self-defense, puts a hair from the home invasion under the microscope. The entire pulp of its follicle is attached, its integrity uncompromised, suggesting a struggle. He presses the man to re-tell his story, needling him about the details, and finally, admits that there was a scuffle. He stepped on the man's sneaker, pulling it off. He then shot him in self-defense, panicked, and then put the sneaker back on the victim.

Warrick relays this revised story to Grissom, who is in the middle of conducting a blunt force trauma experiment involving a golf club, a mannequin's head, and a pint of

Holly's blood. Grissom reminds him that witnesses, perps, and victims all lie, but the evidence always speaks the truth. Warrick combs over the sneaker again and finds a toenail shard.

Holly, at the convenience store, is not faring much better than she did before being dropped off. The proprietor yells at her that she is disrupting business and alarming his customers, and pulls a gun. Catherine arrives just in time to confiscate it, and takes her rookie partner out to lunch. Holly admits over to Catherine that she is not sure why she is there—she feels like she is fulfilling her mother's dreams and not her own.

Meanwhile, Nick gets a call to check on a young woman— possibly a call girl-- who passed out behind the wheel of her car. There is no evidence of criminal activity, however when the working girl comes to he sends her to the hospital just in case.

Brass thinks that the toenail shard does not warrant a warrant, but Warrick goes over his head to Judge Cohen. The judge says that if Warrick places a $5000 bet for him he'll give Warrick a blank warrant to search the premises.

The suicide-turned murder case takes a turn when lab tech Charlotte Meridan shows Grissom a fingerprint from the suicide tape recorder. The print contains red latex flakes laced with lecithin, a common ingredient in cooking sprays. The print also has a match-- a Paul Millander, a local Halloween wholesaler who readily admits the print could be his. His best-selling item is a rubber hand, and his own hand was the mould for it.

Nick is called to the hospital by a Dr. Leever who notes that six call girls have shown up in the last two nights, all knocked unconscious. Nick confronts the girl he found asleep at the wheel of the car. She is given a choice: tell him what the girls are using to knock the guys unconscious and return Larry's wedding band and wallet, or face attempted manslaughter charge. The finds the former option more appealing than the latter, and gives him a bottle of Scopolamine, an anti-motion sickness drug.

Brass has learned that Warrick went over his head for the warrant, and takes him off that particular case. He is now assigned to shadow Holly and audit her work. He goes with her to a home robbery scene, and sends her in alone so he can place Judge Cohen's $5,000 on the wrong team.

Grissom, warrant in hand, goes to the home invasion to the husband for toenail clippings. The man has just given himself something of a pedicure and flushed the clippings down the toilet, so Grissom then returns with an ALS (Alternative Light Source). This handy gadget picks out items that the naked eye can't see, using an ultraviolet light. It reveals a nail fragment whose striations match those on the shard found in the victim's sneaker.

The homeowner, as it turns out, had put on the victim's sneaker and kicked the door with it to support his story that the unwelcome houseguest had tried to break in the door. Warrick shows up to watch the husband being led away.

Holly is busy dusting the scene when a strange man enters, claiming to be a neighbor. She tells him the situation is under control and turns around to go back to work. He pulls a gun on her when her back is turned. As the team celebrates Nick's promotion to CSI 3 Brass interrupts to tell them that Holly has been shot, and he is putting Warrick on administrative leave pending a full investigation.

Memorable Quotes

Grissom (To Holly Gribbs): We scrutinize the crime scene. Collect the evidence. Recreate what had happened without ever been there. It's pretty cool actually.

Holly: There were...bodies. I could feel them...breathing...

Grissom (chuckling): It's okay, Holly. It's all right.

(Grissom turns around to yell at the bodies through the door)

Grissom: You assholes!

(Holly laughs)

Grissom: There. Okay?

Brass: Suicide.

Grissom: You think so, huh?

Brass: You got the sleeping bag for easy cleanup, the bathtub to catch the bullet, open window so the stench alerts the neighbors ... god bless him.

Grissom: Pupa, stage three.

Brass: English. I'm not an entomologist.

Grissom: It's the third stage of larva metamorphosis. This guy's been dead seven days. (Grissom puts the larva into a container)

Brass: That's a maggot, and he stinks. Oh, good, it's almost 11:00. Maybe if I'm lucky I can break out of here in time for a shot at the first rack of the Krispy Kreme.

(Grissom plays suicide tape for Royce Harmon's Mom and Sister)

Grissom: We are so sorry about this Mrs. Harmon. I can only imagine how difficult this must be for you.

Mrs. Harmon: No, you don't understand. This is his picture, but that's not my son's voice.

Warrick: Twenty bucks, by the end of shift, I'm the man.

Nick: Is there anything you won't bet on?

Warrick: Nah. It's college football season, man. I won eight of ten this weekend. Kilt 'em. Outside the Huskers and them punk-ass Irish, I'm up about four G's.

Nick: Hmm, what's the line on us?

Warrick: On us? I'm like Tiger, man! I'm heavily favored.

Holly Gribbs (To Grissom): No offence, but I don't want to eat anything that's been in this office.

(Catherine enters the store with her gun drawn)

Catherine: Gun down!

Store Owner: What? I'm getting robbed again?

Catherine: Everything okay?

Holly Gribbs: Yes, ma'am.

(Catherine radios in everything's fine)

Catherine: You the new girl?

Holly Gribbs: Yeah. Hi, I'm Holly Gribbs.

Catherine: Thanks. I'm Catherine Willows.

Store Owner: And I'm Lesley Stahl. Look, let's forget the formalities. Which one of you people's gonna clean my counter here?

Catherine: Let me tell you something, Lady--if you don't care about catching the suspect neither do we. We're out of here. You can pick your gun up tomorrow.

(They are now walking towards the door)

Holly Gribbs (whispers): You can do that?

Catherine (scoffs): No.

Grissom: Forget about making a hundred, forget about the victim, forget about the suspect and focus on the only thing that can't lie: the evidence. Follow the reason we're having this conversation.

Warrick: (nods) Follow the shoe.

Catherine: What do you think?

Warrick: Oh, he's lying. That's why I took this job. I can always tell when whitey's talking out his ass. It's a gift.

Brass: You're the fifth person I've been forced to

hire. We're the number two crime lab in the country. We solve crimes most labs render unsolvable. Now what makes you think you belong here?

(Holly glances at Grissom. When it's apparent that he's not going to answer for her, Holly turns back to Brass)

Holly Gribbs: Sir, with all due respect I thought the key to being a lucid crime scene investigator was to reserve judgment until the evidence vindicates or eliminates assumption.

Holly Gribbs: You're prejudging me. I graduated with honors in criminal

justice at UNLV.

Brass (flippantly): Yeah, so?

Holly Gribbs: That's not fair.

Brass: Fair? Well, you think putting a juiced-in Lieutenant's daughter on this shift is fair? You know, I've been in the field 22 years. I've seen it

all. I've seen people like you come and go, and you know what? They don't amount to nothing but headaches and bad press. Dismissed. Holly Gribbs: Fine. (She leaves)

Grissom: Think you got through to her?

Brass: You're scheduled to appear at an autopsy at 12:30 A.M. They're cutting up that bozo put a hole in his chest. Take her

with. I think every new hire should experience an autopsy on their first night.

Grissom: Morning. Gil Grissom, forensics. I'm taking over the case for Warrick Brown. Mind if I come in?

Husband: (sighs) How can I help you?

Grissom: I need to give you a pedicure.

Husband: Come again?

Grissom: (ponders) If latex rubber and cooking spray went on a blind date, how would the night end?

Charlotte: A lot better than ours did.

Grissom: I know, Pink Floyd's not your thing.

Charlotte: I have on cowboy boots. I work in a lab. What makes you think "Dark Side of the Moon" synched to the Wizard of Oz is going to warm my damn barn?

Grissom: I just thought it'd be something different.

Charlotte: You want to be different? Pin me up against a wall; lay one on me like you mean it.

Charlotte: You're slacking, pal.

Grissom: How long till we get a hit?

Charlotte: It could be four minutes, could be four days but you can bet your ass she'll give you something. She always does.

Grissom: "Pin you against a wall?"

(Grissom casts Charlotte a sideways glance)

Dr. Klausbach: (to Grissom, referring to Holly) She is cute.

Royce Harmon : (voiceover) My name is Royce Harmon. I reside at 7642 Carpenter Street, Las Vegas, Nevada. I am 41 years of age ... and I'm going to kill myself.

Holly Gribbs: Look, um, I got to be honest. This isn't me. I was pushed into it by my mom. She's a Lieutenant in Traffic. She's never going to get out of
traffic so, um, I'm fulfilling her dreams, not mine.

Catherine: I can sit here and I can baby you and I can tell you to quit but I'm not going to do that, because I really love my job. We're just a bunch of kids that are getting paid to work on puzzles. Sometimes there's a piece that's missing. Sometimes we solve it in one night.

Holly Gribbs: So you think I should stick with it?

Catherine: Stick with it? The cops? Forget it. They wouldn't know fingerprints from paw prints and the detectives...chase the lie. We solve. We restore peace of mind. And when you're a victim, that's everything. Stick it out. At least until you solve your first. And after that, if you don't feel like King Kong on cocaine, then you can quit. But if you stay, with my right hand to God, you will never regret it.

Sargent O'Riley: (Describing Brass and Grissom) Here comes the nerd squad.

Greg (Holding a swab Nick gave him): So this is it, huh? The 8,000-dollar Q-Tip.

Nick: Well, you're the chemist. I just need to know what knocked the old man out.

Greg: In 20 seconds, this'll give us a complete chemical breakdown right down to the atom. But, I've got to warn you, oral swabs don't always read right. Vaginal swabs? No problem. Anal swabs? Money.

Nick: Anal swabs?

Greg: Anal swabs. (Pauses and sits down) Ouch.

Grissom (To Warrick): Yes, you had him and the minute you started thinking about yourself instead of the case, you lost him. There is no room for subjectivity in this department, Warrick. You know that. We handle each case objectively without presupposition regardless of race, color, creed, or bubble gum flavor.

Grissom: I need you to roll up your sleeve and give me a pint of your blood

Holly Gribbs: What for?

Grissom: It's customary for all new hires.

Holly Gribbs: Why?

Grissom: So many reasons.

Warrick: Whose blood is it?

Grissom: The new girl. Want to donate?

Warrick: Hell, no.

Grissom: You gotta breathe through your ears, Gribbs

Cool Change

This is the second episode of the first season of CSI Las Vegas.

Synopsis

A rather down-trodden, weathered-looking man is pumping coins into the Hotel Monaco's Giga-Millions slot machine. He steps away, and a tourist named Jamie Smith, goads her boyfriend, Ted Sallenger, into taking the $40 million pull.

Once he has been upgraded to the presidential suite and has gotten settled in, Sallenger then tells Jamie to get lost. As he enjoys his sumptuous surroundings, there is a knock at the door and an offer for room service. The next thing we see is Sallenger's body splattered on the pavement.

Grissom, when he arrives at the scene, immediately fixates on the fact that Sallenger was still wearing his glasses at the time of his death. This, to him, indicates it was not a suicide.

At the lab, Holly Gribbs' shooting is making waves. Captain Brass is demoted back down to Homicide and Grissom is now made the head of the night shift. He then announces that he is bringing in a Sara Sidle from San Francisco to handle the internal investigation into Warrick's alleged misconduct.

Back at the Monaco, Dr Jenna WilGregs points out shards of black glass in Sallenger's forearms, a telltale sign of a struggle. Grissom and Nick, after gaining entry to his room, find a broken champagne bottle, and blood leading to a bloody towel. The first suspect, Jamie, is brought in for questioning and admits that she did throw the champagne bottle at Ted, but that then he left and didn't return. Her story checks out, so they go to the roof. On the Monaco's roof, Grissom uses three dummies to determine to whether he fell, jumped, or was pushed, and concluded that he was pushed.

Sara Sidle from San Fransisco emerges to help Catherine solve Holly's case, but Catherine is not really thrilled to have been assigned a partner. Sara asks where she might be able to find Warrick and Catherine directs her to Blue Diamond Road.

Grissom and Nick watch a surveillance reel of the casino floor to see what exactly happened when Sallenger won the $40 millions. They find that a man named Red Carlton had been there for over eleven hours, and they easily track him down to another slot machine. Noticing stains on his pants that match the sticky substance that coats hotel roofs to lower heating bills, he has Carlton arrested for conspiracy to commit murder.

Warrick, meanwhile, has his own problems. Having placed Judge Cohen's bet on the wrong team, Warrick owes him $10,000 and has one hour to come up with it. Though he is winning at blackjack (because he is counting cards) when Sara finds him, and she asks where he was when Holly was shot, accusing him of taking off to place a bet. He tells her that on the night of Holly's shooting he went out for coffee. He said there was an officer at the scene, so he wasn't worried about Holly. Plus, as a rookie, he was left alone countless times himself. Sara then informs him that Holly died on the operating table 20 minutes ago.

Progress is made on the case when ballistics tech Bobby Dawson tells Catherine that Holly was shot with her own gun. Even more progress is made when a pager found on the scene begins to ring. She calls the pager's owner and manages to convince him to meet with her.

At the Monaco, Carlton admits to having had a few drinks with Sallenger, but didn't kill him. Devastated that he'd put his life savings into a slot machine, only to lose a moment later, he claims that he went up to the roof alone planning to end it but then changed his mind.

At the Three Aces Motel, Brass and LVPD burst in on Jerrod Cooper, who is the pager's owner. As he's put in cuffs, Catherine notices a nasty scratch on his cheek, and immediately dashes to the morgue so she can collect the samples from under Holly's fingernails.

While Nick and Grissom find no roof dust on Sallenger's shoes, they do find fibers on the stem of his watch. Doctor WilGregs then shows Grissom a diamond-shaped contusion in Sallinger's skull and claims that it was the contusion that killed him. He was dead when he was pushed. Nick returns to the suite and finds a brass candlestick with a large diamond shape on one side. He then applies Crystal Violet to the balcony. Soon it reveals a large bloodstain along with prints of a hand and two knees, previously invisible.

Finally, they put the pieces together and arrest Jamie: after leaving Carlton, Sallenger returned to the suite. There, Jamie hit him with the candle stick. She then dragged him toward the balcony, his watch collecting carpet fibers along the way. Then she heaved him over the edge.

Holly's case is also getting closer to being solved: Greg tells Catherine & Sara that Cooper's DNA matches the samples scraped from beneath Holly's nails. The pieces on this case too are put together: they struggled, Cooper grabbed her weapon, and shot her. But Holly had managed to grab his pager and throw it under the couch, possibly purposefully leaving a clue.

Warrick returns to the lab to talk to Grissom, who ready to let him go for violating procedures. At the last moment, he has a change of heart. "I already lost one good person today," he says, "I don't want to lose another."

Memorable Quotes

Nick: How do you know all this stuff?
Grissom: It's our job to know stuff.

Catherine: Wait a minute. Uh, you-you can't give him the Holly case. I mean, all due respect, Nick. I want this one.
Grissom: Nicky is the only one that didn't have any personal contact with Holly. I don't want you on this, Cath.
Catherine: Why?
Grissom: Because you're emotionally involved.

Catherine: Yeah. She was going to walk. I convinced her to stay. If anyone's to blame here, it's me, and I want this case. (Catherine grabs the assignment sheet from Nick) Fire me.

Grissom: I'm not firing anybody. Look. I know we're pulling a double. We're on edge 'cause of Holly. I just want everyone to stay calm and to do their jobs for the next ten hours. And for now, we're short of help. So I'm bringing in Sara Sidle to give us a hand.

Catherine: Sara Sidle?

Warrick: Who's that?

Grissom: She's a CSI out of San Francisco. She's a friend of mine; someone I trust. She's going to handle our internal investigation and I want to keep this in-house. I don't want I.A. involved. Catherine: Great, that's just what we need: somebody sniffing around.

Sara: Mind if I get a soda?

(Catherine looks at her confused. Sara indicates the refrigerator behind Catherine)

Catherine: Oh, yeah. Sorry. (moves)

Sara: You want one?

Catherine: Is there anything in there with alcohol?

Sara: Root beer.

Catherine: No.

Sara: You were playing $100 on every spot. You have a system?

Warrick: I'm counting cards.

Sara: Isn't that illegal?

Warrick: Not if you do the math in your head.

Sara: You play anything else?

Warrick: I bet sports from time to time.

Sara: So...let me get this straight. You were assigned by Brass to shadow a trainee, a robbery comes up on M.L.K, and you go for coffee.

Warrick: An officer was there.

Sara: So, you felt safe to leave? Do you know the policies and procedures for clearing a scene?

Warrick: Yes.

Sara: Then, why'd you leave? I mean, what was so important that you had to rush out of there?

Warrick: I told you. I went for coffee.

Sara: Was that before or after you made your bets? Sunday...Vegas...NFL football... guy like you...come on, you trying to tell me that you didn't make a little pit stop? (Warrick doesn't say anything) Look at me. Did you log on...tell dispatch where you were going?

Warrick: Do you know how many times I've been left alone at a crime scene when I was a rookie?

Sara: Yeah, well, this time is different.

Warrick: Yeah, why's that?

Sara: Holly Gribbs died on the operating table twenty minutes ago.

Grissom: Was he in town with anybody?

Detective Barns: His girlfriend. She's upstairs in police custody. Do you want to talk to her?

Grissom: Not yet. Right now, I want to talk to him.

Detective Barns: How do you talk to a dead body?

(Grissom moves in closer to the body and kneels down to look at it)

Grissom: I let him talk to me, actually. In fact, he just spoke. Didn't you hear him? He just told me that he didn't commit suicide.

Detective Barns: No. You-you lost me.

Grisson: This guy fell to his death wearing prescription eyeglasses. Jumpers take their glasses off.

Detective Barns (laughs): You can tell all that just by looking at a pair of eyeglasses?

Grissom: You have no idea.

Catherine: You didn't have to come.

Grissom: I know. I wanted to. In case you need me.

Catherine: I probably do. But this is something I'd rather do alone.

Grissom: Fifteen seconds, you're in, you're out we make a DNA match and it's over, okay?

Catherine: (nods) Okay.

Grisssom: They say I have to let you go. You violated the policies and procedures for clearing a scene. I read Sara's report.

Warrick: I know. I messed up. And Holly's dead. I'm sorry, Gil.

Grissom: I'm sorry, too. I don't want to do this.

Warrick: You got to. You know where I was?

Grissom: I think I have a pretty good idea.

Warrick: I went to lay a bet. I didn't even think I was doing anything wrong. Never occurred to me.

Grissom: It never occurred to me, either. You know what? If I let you go I got to let me go, too. And Catherine ... and Brass. We're all culpable in this. I don't care what the book says. I lost one good person today. I don't want to lose another...here.

Warrick: I won't let you down again.

Nick: Can I ask you a question?

Jamie: Sure.

Nick: How are you so cool? You took someone's life. Don't you care?

Jamie: No.

Grissom: Deputy, we're going to have her arrested.

Jamie (to Grissom): So, could I ask you a question?

Grissom: Maybe.

Jamie: All that stuff you rattled off. How'd you know about all that?

Grissom: Your boyfriend told me.

Grissom: All right, Nick. Standing by for operation Norman. Let him fly.

Grissom (To Crowd): Yes, yes. (Takes a photo of the first dummy, to himself) "Norman pushed." (Takes a photo of the second dummy) "Norman jumped." (Takes a picture of the third dummy) "Norman fell."

Sara: Wouldn't you if you were married to Mrs. Roper? (Smiles)

Grissom: I don't even have to turn around. Sara Sidle.

Sara: It's me. Still tossing simulation dummies? There are other ways to tell, you know?

Grissom: How? Computer simulation? No thanks. I'm a scientist I like to see it. Newton dropped the apple, I drop dummies.

Sara: You're old school.

Grissom: Exactly. And this guy was pushed.

(Brass gets demoted to homicide, which puts Grissom in charge)

Grissom: You got any advice for me?

Brass: Yeah, cover your ass ... and hide. They're all yours, pal.

Grissom: God Sara, I have so many unanswered whys.

Sara: There's only one why that matters now, why did Warrick Brown leave that scene?

Sara: Do you know where I can find Catherine Willows?

Catherine: She's out in the field. Let me guess, Sara Sidle?

Sara: I know who I am. I think you're a little confused.

Sara: What are you gonna say? "Hi, I'm a Criminalist. I was in the neighborhood..."

Catherine: Shh. It's ringing.

Jerrod Cooper (From phone): Hello?

Catherine: Oh, hey.

Jerrod Cooper: Who's this? I just dialed my own damn beeper.

Catherine: It's my beeper now. I found it.

Jerrod Cooper: It ain't yours. That's my beeper. I do a lot of business on that beeper.

Catherine: What kinda business?

Jerrod Cooper: Oh, you know. Slangin' a little somethin' somethin'.

Catherine: Oh, a little somethin' somethin'. Or maybe a little bling-bling?

Jerrod Cooper: What do you know about a little bling-bling?

Catherine: Invite me over to your crib, baby. You might find out.

Jerrod Cooper: Three Aces Motel. Room 202.

Catherine: Three Aces Motel, room 202. See you soon. Did I just do that?

Sara: So what's a "bling bling"?

Catherine: Got me.

Grissom: (Laughing) Jacks or better. You're under arrest.

Suspect: Oh yeah? What for?

Grissom: First degree murder.

Suspect: Oh. On what grounds?

Grissom: Roof dust.

Crate and Burial

This is the third episode of the first season of CSI Las Vegas.

Synopsis

A woman named Laura Garas is shown suffering the doubtlessly horrible fate of being buried alive while pleading and screaming for help. A recorded message instructs the listener to "Bring two million in hundreds to Charleston and Third in three hours or your wife dies. Stop me from taking the money she still dies."

At the Garas home, Brass attempts to convince Laura's husband, Jack, that he should not succumb to his panic and pay the ransom. Meanwhile, Grissom and Nick scrutinize the message for clues that would give away the whereabouts of the speaker or the wife. Observing a gap of silence and a low, humming, buzzing sound, they guess that the message was recorded in desert near power lines.

Sara identifies the site of Laura's abduction and carefully inspects it. There are a myriad of" points of disturbance" that point to a heated struggle. When Grissom joins her, he notices dirt on the bedroom carpet and a handkerchief lying on the ground, doused in Halothane - a liquid anesthetic.

Meanwhile, Catherine and Warrick have been sent to investigate the hit and run of young woman named Renda Harris, who was knocked off her scooter. Finding little of interest on the scooter or at the scene, they return to the lab, where Doctor WilGregs shows them a partial license plate number that has been imprinted on her body in a bruise.

As for Laura Garas: an analysis of the dirt from the Garas home reveals traces of gold and cyanide. This is somewhat of a breakthrough: Grissom explains that miners use cyanide powder to draw gold to the surface. Unable to dissuade Jack Garas from paying the ransom, Brass trails him to the drop site, where Garas leaves a gym bag filled with cash into a trash can. When a young man in a baseball cap eventually fishes it out of the trash, the police surround him.

At the same time, Grissom and Sara comb the desert with an infrared camera until they see the silhouette of a person squirming under the surface of the cracked, dry earth. Frantically, they dig until Laura is freed from her grave.

A hit on the partial license plate number leads Catherine and Warrick to the home of Charles Moore, a distinguished seventy-three-year-old. Although he claims his car was stolen, a perfunctory search finds it in the garage. Moore confesses that he was behind the wheel and accidentally hit Renda.

When Grissom interviews Laura Garas at the hospital, she remembers little. She said she was grabbed from behind in the hallway of her home and something was clamped over her mouth. Laura can't remember anything about her assailant. Grissom matches DNA from the duct tape used to cover her mouth to DNA left at the drop off site. The two samples are DNA from one Chip Rundle, Jack Garas' personal trainer. Further incriminating him are the prints he left on Lara's makeshift coffin. Rundle manages to evade arrest by claiming that his prints are on the crate because he'd helped Jack move them. Rundle is released, but Brass has recorded the interrogation for comparison with the ransom message.

Meanwhile, Catherine and Warrick check out Moore's car. Noticing that the stereo is set to blast a local hip hop station. After questioning, Mr. Moore admits that after hitting Renda, he'd banged his head so his grandson James drove him home.

Rundle's fate is becoming more and more certain as his voice is matched with that on the ransom tape. Sara, reviewing the evidence collected from Rundle's truck, notes that fibers from the seat's sheepskin cover were found on the back of Laura's sleeves. A blood test confirms that Laura never was exposed to the halothane. Brass enters, saying Rundle now wants to make a deal, but Grissom wants to make sure that Rundle hands over his accomplice, Laura, in the making of the deal.

Taking a closer look at Charles Moore's car, Catherine retrieves a small piece of tooth embedded in the steering wheel. When they ask to see his teeth he plucks out an entire set of dentures, so they arrest his grandson instead.

Laura, when being questioned, denies that Rundle is her accomplice, and that she has ever had any kind of relationship with him. Nick plays three versions of the ransom recording. The final has isolated and magnified the previously undetectable sound of Laura saying, "Hurry up, Chip!" As Laura is taken away, an angry, surprised, and saddened Jack Garas asks Grissom why his wife didn't just give Rundle up. "Self Preservsation," Grissom explains. "If she rats on him, she rats on herself."

Memorable Quotes

Grissom: I tend not to believe people. People lie. The evidence doesn't lie.

Sara: You're standing in my crime scene.

Nick: No. You're in mine.

(Nick smiles and turns to walk out of the house)

Sara : You're doing audio? I wanted that.

Nick: I outrank you.

Sara: Technicality. Who did Grissom handpick to work here?

Mr. Garris: You guys have got to move!

Grissom: Mr Garris? It's my experience that in situations like this, if you want to go fast, go slow.

Catherine: All we got is some paint that's going to match about twenty million other vehicles.

Warrick: Yeah.

Catherine: Bastard.

Sara: Excuse me. Is my evaluation interrupting you?

Grissom: No, no, no. I barely heard you.

Sara: Glad I have a healthy ego.

Grissom: People leave us clues, Nick. They speak to us in thousands of different ways. It's our job to make sure we've tried to hear every single thing they've said.

Grissom (smiling): You have to see the birthday present I got for your daughter.

Sara: What's the rule? How long do I have to be here before I start kicking in for gifts?

Catherine: When the spirit moves you, Sara. So, in your case, I guess, never.

Grissom: I got one of these chem labs when I was six. I almost blew up the whole house.

Catherine: I hope you can return it 'cause, uh, Lindsey doesn't want a party.

Grissom: Yeah, what kid doesn't want a party?

Catherine: My kid.

Nick: Hey, Catherine what time's your little girl coming by?

Catherine: She isn't.

Nick: Yeah, but I got her a chem set.

Sara: You keep that; might learn something.

Nick: Stop flirting with me. Cath, really, when's the party?

Catherine: What do I have to do---put it on the bulletin board? There is no party. My daughter doesn't want a party. Is everybody clear on that?

Grissom: We'll play with these later.

Grissom: You any better?

Catherine: What are you talking about?

Grissom: Your little major-minor blowup about Lindsey not wanting a party.

Catherine: Oh, that. Yeah. I'm just afraid that I'm making her weird, you know?

Grissom No.

Catherine: I work 24/7. I have no time for my friends. My daughter rarely sees me having any fun. And, all of a sudden, she doesn't want a party.

Grissom: And that's because of you?

Catherine: Yes. I'm her mother. She mimics me.

Grissom: Well, then she'll be fine. I mean, look at you.

Catherine: You're just saying that to make me feel better.

Grissom: Yeah.

Sara: Hey Grissom....could you come tape me up?

Grissom: I love my work.

Catherine: It shows.

Pledging Mr. Johnson

This is the fourth episode of the first season of CSI Las Vegas.

Synopsis

Two fishermen manage to reel in a dismembered leg, and CSI is called. They discover that the leg was removed after the owner of the leg had died. The body was possibly severed from the leg by a boat propeller. As soon as the police divers pull up the remains from the lake, the body is quickly identified as Wendy Barger, the missing wife of Winston Barger, who didn't even realize she was missing.

Nick and Sara, meanwhile, are assigned to investigate a college suicide. They first start with the deceased's frat brothers. While they seem at first to be helpful, it quickly becomes obvious that they are hiding something. The pair immediately suspects a hazing incident gone awry.

Warrick, meanwhile, has run into Judge Cohen. Judge Cohen is angling for a cover-up in a Henderson rape case. Late at night, after informing Grissom as to what's going on, he meets the judge in a park. Judge Cohen asks him to break the seal on the evidence box, and tamper with the evidence to exonerate him from the rape case. AS soon as he has finished making the request, however, the police converge and arrest him.

Sara and Nick have discovered that James did not indeed die from hanging. He suffocated after raw liver, of all things, was caught in his throat. It seems that as part of a hazing ritual, James had his privates signed by the girlfriend of the frat president. The frat president, furious, instituted the raw liver hazing situation, which he didn't expect James to survive. The president is booked on Murder   in   the   First   Degree.

Grissom, meanwhile, re-enacts Wendy's accident in a tub to see how she could have met her end. Catherine goes on foot to find the boat that Wendy must have fallen out of. At first foul play is suspected but upon close examination, it is concluded that the boat simply ran out of gas, and when Wendy attempted to start the motor, she wrenched her shoulder, fell, cracked her skull and fell over the side.

They arrive at Wendy's former residence too late. Her widowed husband, thinking that his friend Phil Swelco is responsible for his wife's death, has shot him to death.

Memorable Quotes

Catherine: Well...(sighs)...I guess we better go talk to the husband. I mean, unless you think I'm going to compromise the integrity of the case again. (she gets up)

Grissom: Look, could we have a truce?

Catherine: I would love to.

Grissom: Good. (he helps her out of the boat) But let me do all the talking to the husband and the boyfriend.

Catherine (shakes her head, quietly): He had to say it.

Grissom: Get in the boat. Pull the engine cord.

Catherine: What?

Grissom: Get in the boat.

Catherine: Why?

Grissom: Just indulge me, please?

Catherine: There's no gas. It's not gonna start.

Grissom: That's not the point.

Catherine (sighs): As long as there is one

Catherine: New pet?

Grissom: The African Red Baboon Tarantula---the most feared of all arachnids. But basically harmless.

Catherine: Yeah, well just keep the lid on it, okay?

Grissom: I think you scared him. All his hairs are standing up.

Catherine: If you're through amusing yourself I have some news on the boat.

Grissom: Was it at the Marina?

Catherine: What do you think?

Grissom: My spider sense says it wasn't.

Catherine: Right. We need to find the boa

Catherine: What do you think the chances are she was seeing somebody else?

Grissom: You were married. You tell me.

Catherine: Very good to excellent.

Grissom: How's it look for prints?

Dr. WilGregs: Her skin's shriveled like a shar-pei. No pressure, no prints.

(Grissom looks expectantly at Catherine. Catherine knows that look)

Catherine: No. No way, use your own hand.

Grissom: Come on, Catherine, my hand's too big.

Catherine (firmly): No!

Grissom: It's the only way we can print her. Her skin on your hand should fit like a leather glove. (Grissom reaches for the hand and a knife. Catherine watches as Grissom takes the skin off of the hand. When he finishes, he looks up at Catherine and extends his hand to her) May I take your hand? (Catherine puts her hand in Grissom's and he leads her to the table where the fingerprint kit is. Although we don't see it, Grissom puts the dead woman's skin on Catherine's hand) On behalf of the decedent I thank you. (He takes the fingerprint)

Catherine: Umm...

Grissom: I think we're going to know who she is by lunchtime.

Sara: What's that smell?

Nick: I'm nuking a burrito.

Sara: Mmm, junk food and radiation.. good combo!

Greg: Hey, Grissom. I hear Catherine beat you to the boat.

Grissom: We work as a team. We're not competing.

Greg: Okay. But, ah, she found it first. Right?

Grissom: "Two roads diverged in a yellow wood and, sorry I could not travel
both."

Greg: Robert Frost.

Grissom: Very good, Greg.

Greg: Thanks.

Grissom: But actually, in this case, Mr. Frost does not apply. When you have a partner you each take a road. That's how you find a missing boat.

Greg: Come on. Level with me. Who do you think killed her.. the husband or boyfriend?

Grissom: And you've narrowed it down to just two suspects?

Greg: Actually, you did. You see, my second week at CSI, you told me that when a cheating spouse is murdered there are always two suspects at the top of the list: The lover and the betrayed.

Grissom: I told you this?

Greg: Mm-hmm. You see, I'm thinking that the husband caught Wendy with the boyfriend and when she left his house, he killed her in a jealous rage.

Grissom: And this theory is based on...?

Greg: Nothing. I'm just trying to help.

Grissom: I'm going to the garage to meet Catherine. You keep thinking, Butch. That's what you're good at.

Greg: Hey. If this theory checks out, uh maybe we should talk about a raise.

Grissom (laughing): Yeah

Catherine: I can tell you first hand, when you don't cheat, you don't suspect.

Brass: Oh, man, I wish I had been married to you.

Catherine: Not a chance

Catherine: You're right, you know. I should be just like you. Alone in my hermetically sealed condo, watching Discovery on the big screen, working genius-level crossword puzzles.

But no relationships, no chance any will slop over into a case. Yeah, right. I want to be just like you.

Grissom: Technically it's a townhouse. And the crosswords are advanced, not genius. But you're right, I'm deficient in a lot of ways. But I never screw up one of my cases with personal stuff.

Catherine: Grissom...what personal stuff?

Warrick: Let me guess. Radiohead or Rage Against the Machine?

Greg: Actually, it's an audio book on restriction enzyme analysis and DNA typing. PCR fingerprinting. Choice.

Warrick: Right.

(As they walk by Greg sees Grissom in the garage)

Greg: What's Grissom doing in the garage?

Warrick: Oh, he's working that Wendy Barger case -- you know, the floater?

Greg: Oh.

Warrick: Only clue he's got is a missing boat, which sucks because... it's missing.

Greg (chuckles): He thinks he's going to find it in a bathtub?

Warrick: It's a simulation tank. He's re-creating the conditions the night she died. Body was dumped, like, a half mile from Calville Bay. They think the
boat must have drifted with the currents.

Greg: And let me guess, Catherine got bored.

Warrick: Well, you know Grissom. Shortest distance between two points is

science. And for Catherine, it's pounding the pavement.

Brass: You're under arrest for obstructing justice, tampering with state's evidence, and violating seven articles of being scumbag

Nick: I can't believe I used to live in a place like this.

Sara: And here I had all this respect for you

Dr. WilGregs: The leg was severed post-mortem.

Catherine: Well, that's good news.

Dr. WilGregs: How do you figure?

Catherine: Would you want to be alive while your leg's being cut o

Friends and Lovers

This is the fifth episode of the first season of CSI Las Vegas.

Synopsis

In the desert, two naked boys are running frantically, looking over their shoulders as they try to escape from the as-of-yet unrevealed person or persons that are pursuing them, Later, Grissom and Warrick look at naked body whose positioning leads Grissom to believe he was running and looking over his shoulder at his time of death. The cause of death is listed simply as fear—he was chased to death. In the morgue, a careful analysis yields jimsonweed in the boy's system.

Sara, assigned to deal with a body that appeared in a dumpster, arrives at the scene to discover that the body had been embalmed. She runs the prints at the lab, and finds out that the woman was buried a week ago.

Catherine and Nick arrive at their assignment: to investigate a body found at a school. The dead man was, at one time, the Dean of the school, and died of blunt force trauma to the head. The suspect is Kit Armstrong, the founder of the school, who also called in the death. Her story is that the dean attacked her, and that she hit him once on the head to get him to stop. Catherine tells her that the body shows that he was struck on the head more than once and Catherine admits that she's not entirely sure what exactly happened. .

Meanwhile, Brass questions Bobby, a friend of the dead boy in the desert. Bobby gives them some useful information: he says that the last time he saw Eric was at midnight at a rave they were at together. Brass tells him that they have a body that might be Eric and Bobby identifies him as such. Warrick confirms that jimsonweed was not only found in the maggots infesting the body, but in the body itself, as well as trace elements of aluminum in his nose. The aluminum is unexplainable, but Grissom comments that this would make whoever ingested it "blind as a bat, red as a beet and mad as a hatter." Bobby says he now remembers that Eric took jimsonweed, and that the DJ sold it to him.

Catherine and Nick carefully examine the room where the dean was found. The spattering of the blood is in a pattern that indicates that the Dean was hit three times, he died on the floor, and that someone besides the Dean and Mrs. Armstrong was in the room when the attack occurred.

Sara, trying to figure out how a woman could show up in a dumpster a week after being put in the ground, talks to a funeral arranger. They excavate the grave, but there's no casket there; the director suggests that a grave robber could not only have stolen jewelry from the deceased, but stolen the casket as well. As Sarah later discovers, eternity isn't cheap: caskets can be tens of thousands of dollars, and they only are used by one person so there's no chance of splitting the bill.

Catherine, Nick and an officer talk to Armstrong again, telling her that they know someone else was in the room. Armstrong identifies that person as Julia Easton, who says that she was a witness for the harassment, and was standing in the doorway. Nick tells her that they've re-enacted the crime, and it appears as though he was held down by one person while another beat him.

At a rave in the desert, Grissom, Warrick, Brass, and Bobby find the guy that sold Eric the jimsonweed. Ethan, the seller, invites them to search his car, taking a blasé attitude towards the whole thing since jimsonweed doesn't carry a very heavy sentence, if any. Grissom finds some seeds in the car, and once reexamined, seeds are found in Eric's body. He tries to match them up to the ones in the car, hoping that this may be a piece of the puzzle leading to the story behind Eric's murder. Still, this is not enough to convict Ethan of murder so he is released.

Catherine and Nick, unsatisfied with their work on the case and the evidence they've gathered, ask to see the clothes Julia was wearing at the time of the assault, and examine a bloody handprint on the scene, unique because of the odd angle of the pinky finger. Julia tells them that she burned the clothes because the blood wouldn't come out.

Grissom tells Bobby that Eric didn't die because of the tea, and while Bobby listens he scratches furiously at his arm. When asked, he says that he thinks he has a spider bite and shows it to Grissom. Grissom, wondering if the insect bite is actually a human bite, requests a bite plate to be made of Eric's teeth. Warrick comes in with some fireworks residue from the party in the desert; Bobby works at a fireworks place.

The bloody handprint discovered in a more thorough examination of the Dean's final resting place matches Julia's. Catherine speculates that Julia held Dean Woods down while Kit Armstrong killed him, and both women refuse to volunteer more information as they are arrested. Nick is satisfied that they have enough evidence to build a case but Catherine isn't satisfied.

Sara asks the funeral director if he's selling time-share coffins, and gets him to reiterate that each coffin is only used for one person. She asks him about the prints on the plastic that was used to wrap the body, and he gets quiet, finally telling her that he's in a cutthroat business and he did what he had to do to make a profit. Sara tells him that he has to pay back the money for the coffin, and have the body reburied and then the case will go to the D.A.

Under pressure, Kit and Julia fill in the details of the story: they were lesbians, and the Dean threatened to out them. Kit, the founder of the school, feared that parents would pull their children out of her school, and that there would be a media circus that would permanently damage her school's reputation. The dean had to go.

Brass questions Bobby, who can't remember anything after drinking the jimsonweed tea. Warrick Eric was naked because the jimsonweed convinced him that he was hot, and afraid of the sun, and having auditory hallucinations. They allege that Bobby, also under the influence and suffering from similar hallucinations, killed his friend. Bobby's lawyer says that it's all conjecture and Grissom matches the bite plate made of Eric's mouth to the bite mark on Bobby's arm. The lawyer says they'll plead diminished capacity; Bobby says he doesn't care what happens to him, because he killed his best friend.

Warrick and Grissom sit outside and drink coffee; Bobby is taken away by officers. Grissom leaves, and rides the roller coaster at New York, New York.

Memorable Quotes

Warrick: Where you going?
Grissom: Away

Kimberley Cassano: Well, I can tell you right now we're going to plead diminished capacity.
Grissom: Good, I hope you win.
Bobby: It doesn't matter.
Kimberley Cassano: Bobby, it's the difference between prison and a hospital.
Bobby: You don't understand. I don't care what happens to me. I killed my best friend

Grissom: Let me tell you something, Humbert. You're twice the age of these kids and most of them couldn't find their ass with a map. You prey on innocent children concocting god-knows-what from god-knows-where selling Russian roulette in a bottle and you think we came all the way out here to bust you for

"possession", you dumb punk? (beat) I'm gonna get you for murder.

Grissom: You want to know what killed this kid? Benihana the maggots.
Warrick: What the maggots

Grissom: Someone chased this kid to death.

Nick: It's our job to know how. You heard Grissom: the more "how" the less "why". The less the "how" the more the "why".
Catherine: Hey, Nick. Grissom's not always right. Do yourself a favor ; think for yourself. I mean that as a friend, okay?

Grissom: I was flying to a seminar in New Hampshire a couple of summers ago. I was sitting in the plane next to a Philosophy Professor from Harvard. He told me this story about how every morning he takes a leak right after his three-hour philosophy class. He flushed the toilet there'd be this tiny brown spider fighting for its life against the swirling water. He came back the next day, flush. Same spiders, clawing its way back from oblivion. A week goes by, he decides to liberate the spider. Grabs a paper towel, Scoops him up and sets him on the floor in the corner of the stall. Comes back the next day and what do you think happened to the spider?

Warrick: Dead.

Grissom: On his back, eight legs up. Why? Because one life imposed itself on another. Right then I realized, where we stand. For the first time I understood our role. We don't impose our will. We don't impose our hopes on the evidence.

Grissom: There are three kinds of people I hate. Men who hit their wives, sexual violation towards children, and the scum who sell death to underage kids

Who Are You?

This is the sixth episode of the first season of CSI Las Vegas.

Synopsis

While investigating a leak underneath a house, a plumber stumbles upon a hand and calls LVPD. Nick and Grissom arrive on the scene and supervise as the body is extracted from the foundation of the house.

Grissom and Nick are assigned the body that was embedded in the foundation of the House, and Sara and Warrick get to investigate a shooting death. The other case assigned to CSI is the rape of an exotic dancer, and Catherine's ex-husband Eddie stands as the sole suspect. She wants to do the preliminary investigation, which Grissom allows though it is a conflict of interest. She watches Eddie through the glass and goes in to talk to him and he claims that he had consensual sex with the woman.

Grissom and Nick examine the skeleton and find it was a woman, that she was stabbed with a curved serrated-edge weapon, and that she most likely knew her attacker. They do a little research and find out that the foundation was poured five years ago by Summercliff Builders.

Meanwhile, Brass introduces Sara and Warrick to Officer Joe Tyner. They learn that there were shots fired and the suspect fled the scene. The suspect then turned the weapon on himself. The cop drew his piece, he said, but never fired. Warrick takes the officer's gun and that of the deceased, Warrick wants to seal off the lot that was the site of the death, but Brass says that they know what happened so it will be unnecessary. Warrick persists, however. He wonders why someone would flee all the way down the strip just to pull over and kill himself. He finds one bullet missing from the officer's gun and Sara comments that taking on the LVPD will cause a lot of waves and ruffle a lot of feathers.

Sara and Nick decide to pursue the matter anyway. They question the officer, who says that the missing bullet is because he doesn't 'top off' which he knows he's not supposed to do. They comment on the fact that his record is rife with complaints of excessive force and IA investigations. Brass, knowing the implications of taking on the LVPD, instructs Warrick and Sara to go out and find the missing bullet. Warrick comments that it's a good thing he sealed off the crime scene despite Brass's disinterest in doing so.

Teri Miller and Grissom, meanwhile, make a mould of the skeleton's face using plaster and paint to figure out what the person may have looked like when alive. Grissom photographs the face and puts it on the local news to see if anyone has any information.

Catherine, meanwhile, feels uneasy about taking on a case wherein her ex husband is accused raping a stripper. Grissom advises her to pass it.

Further investigation of Grissom's skeleton shows that she suffered a hairline fracture to her skull, indicating blunt force trauma. She also had sand and salt in her ear, which indicated that she died at the beach, or just after visiting the beach. The mould of the face, meanwhile, has yielded results: the victim has been identified as Fay Green and her mother, who called the hotline, says that she was athletic and had a boyfriend, Jason Hendler. She says that the police interviewed him when Fay disappeared but found no evidence suggesting that he was in any way involved. She also said she didn't believe that Fay had been to the beach before she died.

April, the rape victim, talks to Detective Evans and Catherine without knowing that Catherine is the ex wife of her alleged rapist. She shares the details of the rape and consents to having a sample taken from under her fingernails.

Sara and Warrick examine the parking lot, and a guy who works valet parking tells them that he saw the officer shoot the guy in the car.

Catherine, though conflicted, has decided to continue working on the rape case. She says that there are some bruises, but Eddie's always been vigorous. Grissom tells her that it's about the evidence, not her feelings on the case or her experiences with the perp.

Greg, examining the sand from the skeleton, corroborates the victim's mother's story. The sand is not from the beach. It was man-made in a rock crusher.

The officer in the shooting case, meanwhile, has learned that a witness has come forward and CSI is investigating the incident. He yells at Warrick and Sara, telling them that they have no idea what it's like to put their life on the line or draw their guns, and is about to attack Warrick, but Grissom and Brass pull him off before any damage is done.

In a Casino restaurant, Catherine and Eddie are having dinner in a major breach of protocol. He says he's happy she's on the case, and adds that he doesn't have a lawyer, because he has her and the truth.

Warrick, determined to continue the shooting investigation examines the car. He finally finds the bullet but it matches the suspect's gun, not the officer's. Re-enaction of the crime demonstrates that the officer couldn't have shot the suspect.

Catherine and a detective go to the strip club and searches April's locker. She finds contraceptive film.

Grissom and Nick go to visit Jason Hendler. He says Fay only lived there for about a month five years ago, but they feel it's worthwhile to search his house nonetheless . They find a fish tank, and a warped floor board, and when Grissom lifts the floor board he finds sand underneath. Grissom says that the tank has been moved, and at some point it broke and there was water and sand on the floor. Later, Nick does some research and learns that Mr. Hendler used to work for the construction company that built the house where they found Fay.

Catherine gets the results from the rape kit and it matches the contraceptive film that the stripper had in her locker. Greg notes that the film has to be inserted prior to sex, and this means that April put it in before she was raped. This of course doesn't necessarily mean that the sex was consensual. It means that at one time, April may have wanted to have sex with Eddie, but it is still possible that she changed her mind and was forced.

April is interviewed again and this time, she is pressured and changes her story. She tells Catherine that Eddie kept promising her things and not delivering so she set him up for rape in hopes that she could extract money from him. Of course, he doesn't have money, but April was led to believe otherwise.

Grissom and Nick return to the Hendler's with a warrant, and re-examine the floor, but the sand has been vacuumed up, and luminal spray reveals nothing. Grissom speculates that Mr. Hendler and Fay had a fight and she got thrown into the fish tank, and then he attacked her, killed her, and buried her, but still doesn't know what the weapon was or have proof. Nick looks at some pictures on the wall and sees rock climbing pictures and recognizes the rock pick as the weapon. Mrs. Hendler goes berserk and draws a gun on Nike. She tells Nick that her husband was engaged to her when he met Fay, and that she killed her. Grissom comes back in and has a gun pointed at Mrs. Hendler. She puts down her gun.

At a park, Catherine watches her daughter play. Eddie arrives and wants to take her out to breakfast to say thank you and to talk but she says no. She says there's nothing to talk about - he cheated on her, and she caught him, and she has a new life now.

Memorable Quotes

Nick (walks in): You brought the foundation of the house to our lab.

Grissom: It's a six-by-three-foot section. When the concrete dried it preserved a partial impression of our Jane Doe. Did you find out anything about the house?

Nick: I pulled the permits. Summercliff was built five years ago on nothing but desert.

Grissom: That would explain why the body was so desiccated.

Nick: House was sold subsequent to completion, so the homeowner isn't a suspect. Homicide is running a missing persons check.

Grissom: Well, if it wasn't for a leaky pipe she might have been down there forever.

Nick: I think our killer was counting on that.

Sara: Both guns are nine millimeter automatics. Brass isn't going to like this.

Warrick: I don't give a damn what Brass likes.

Sara: Like I do? If Tyner's dirty, he goes down. I just know what happens when you piss off the P.D.

Warrick: Yeah, it's war.

Catherine: What do you got for me? I could use a rush.

Grissom: Well, this qualifies: 4-26. But I can't give you the case.

Catherine: Because?

Grissom: Conflict of interest. The alleged rape victim is an exotic dancer.

Catherine: And because I used to be one, I'll be biased?

Grissom: No. The suspect's your ex-husband. He's asking for you, but you can't take it.

Catherine: Just let me do the prelim.

Grissom: All right. Do what you can. But after the preliminary, you pass it off, okay?

Sara: I drive.

Warrick: Picture that.

Brass: So I bet you think I owe you one, huh?

Warrick: We work. We get paid. You don't owe me anything.

Brass (smirks): Fine with me.

Catherine: I'm a forensic scientist.

April Lewis: Scientist... wow. You look so normal.

Catherine: Thanks.

Grissom: I'm sure someone needs closure... and somebody else needs to go to jail.

Grissom: Based on the auricular surface I'd say she died when she was about twenty.

Nick: She?

Grissom: It's in the hips. Pelvic bone is definitely female. You know, for a ladies' man you don't know much about bone structure.

Eddie: When are we going to talk about what happened?

Catherine: What's to talk about? You cheated on me. I caught you.

Greg: So, how many grains of sand in the ocean, huh?

Nick: I don't care about the ocean, just the sand in my skeleton. Can you pinpoint a beach?

Greg: I don't know. I might have to do some field research to find out. You think Grissom would let me go to Hawaii?

Nick: Why don't you ask him yourself?

Grissom: Ask me what?

Greg: Oh, nothing. I, uh ... I was just telling Nick about your sand.

Well, it's not sand. It's not natural anyway. Here, check this out. Now, if this were natural sand, the surface would be smooth. This looks more like Fremont Street on a Saturday night...rough.

Nick: Could the particles be sediment from the concrete where we found her?

Greg: No. No way. I analyzed the mineral content. It's feldspar and quartz. That's crushed gray sandstone. It's man-made, in a rock crusher.

Nick: What does that mean?

Grissom: It means she wasn't killed in Hawaii. (Greg freezes when he realized Grissom heard him before) Other than that, he has no idea.

(Nick laughs)

Nick: Mrs. Hendler, do you and your husband do much rock climbing?

Amy Hendler: Yes. That's what I killed her with.

Detective Evans: You dressed like that?

Catherine (laughs): If you want to call it dressed.

Nick: Ten bucks says the owner sells the house.

Grissom: By law you've got to disclose everything. Three bedrooms, two baths, and a skeleton.

Grissom: So, how's the thing going on Eddie Willows?

Warrick: What thing?

Grissom: The thing that I told Catherine to pass off to you.

Warrick: Oh, good. Um...we just put some stuff through the lab.

Grissom: Get a hold of the DMV?

Warrick: I was just about to.

Grissom: Warrick, why would you call the DMV for a rape case?

Catherine: Okay. I didn't hand it off.

Grissom: Really?

Catherine: I'm sorry, Warrick.

Warrick: If you want me to suave anyone, I got to know the shot.

Catherine: I know. I'm sorry.

Catherine: I'm doing this for Lindsey.

Grissom: You so much as breathe on the evidence, it's contaminated and I end up the bad guy.

Catherine: Eyes, no hands.

Grissom: What's the status?

Catherine: Skin samples from under the women's fingernails are consistent with Ed's. I saw some bruises.

But Eddie's style has always been very... involved. Vigorous.

Grissom (Puzzled): Vigorous.

Warrick: She's trying to tell you Eddie likes it rough.

Catherine: Thank you, Warrick. Eddie said that she was into it.

Grissom: "He said. She said?" It's about the evidence, Catherine. And you may not like where it takes you.

Blood Drops

This is the seventh episode of the first season of CSI Las Vegas..

Synopsis

At a house in the suburban outskirts of Las Vegas, a girl comes bolting out of her house shouting for help.

There are four dead: a mother, father, and two sons. The only family members that have survived the assault are a teenaged girl and her younger sister, who, according to preliminary investigations, couldn't possibly have been responsible. Grissom and a note-taker go in for a walk through. Grissom notes a heavy copper smell in the air, which means that there's a lot of blood, and tells the assistant to breathe through his mouth lest he fall ill from the stench. Upstairs, the father's body is splayed in the hallway, bleeding from multiple stab wounds in the back and neck. The assistant turns faintly green and Grissom releases him from his note taking responsibilities so he can go get sick outside, and, in a stroke of good timing, Sara arrives. There's a blood swirl on the wall, and Sara suggests it could have been some sort of cult murder. They find the mother in her bed, having been stabbed in her sleep. In the boys' bedroom, they find one son dead in bed; the second bed is empty, but when looking at another swirl of blood on the mirror, Grissom sees the second body, between the bed and the wall, with two bloody hand prints on the wall above it.

Grissom tells the police that he needs his entire team to assist in the investigation. Det. O'Reily talks to Tina, the teen-aged daughter, and requests her clothes for examination. Grissom tries to talk to Brenda, the younger sister, but in shock in the back of a police car, she won't answer his questions. As he gets up to leave, she says, "the Buffalo," but doesn't elaborate when pressed. Grissom tells the team that they may not grant interviews. Catherine is to map the scene; Nick and Warrick are to examine the perimeter.

In the house, Grissom checks the kitchen. This is the only room in the house with no blood. Little in the kitchen has been disturbed, indicating that the killer was familiar with the house. A knife is missing. O'Reilly tells Grissom that the media wishes to talk to him but he remains firm that no one should talk to them and tells Sara to take Brenda to the hospital.

The team returns when the sun does so they can check the perimeter. Nick finds a cigarette butt and burnt matches in the flower bed, and Warrick finds tire tracks from a bike in the dirt. Grissom asks Catherine's opinion as to whether a cult is responsible and she seems skeptical at the possibility. Grissom tries to speculate as to how the homicide unfolded. He thinks that the mother was killed first, in bed. Then the father was killed as he ran out of the bedroom to protect the kids. They both agree that whoever was left at the scene is their first suspect: Tina.

Sara complains to Brass that she shouldn't be the one to be looking after Brenda since Catherine is a mother and is bound to have more maternal instincts to offer, but Brass is unsympathetic and tells Sara to take her for a psych eval. Brass and Grissom interview Tina. She tells them that she heard footsteps and hid in the closet. Grissom asks if she has a boyfriend; she says that she's dated a couple of guys, but there are none that she is particularly serious about, and none of them are referred to "Buffalo." Brass comments since she has such a large family, she must be used to hearing footsteps at night. She insists that something about these footsteps were different.

Warrick takes prints of the tire tracks in the garden, and Nick agree that it's bigger than a bicycle but smaller than a motorcycle.

Warrick tells Grissom that the tire treads belong to a '93 scooter, and a kid who lives three blocks away from the crime scene owns one. They are still focused on Tina as the primary suspect but Grissom is concerned that there's no blood at all on Tina's clothes, supporting her claim that she escaped because she heard footsteps and hid.

Ecklie tells Grissom that the Sheriff wants results, and pressures Grissom into letting him take over the case with his own team. Grissom refuses. Warrick interviews the kid who owns the scooter; he says that he doesn't know anything about Tina's parents getting killed, and he doesn't know where the scooter is as he shares it with three other people. Sara, meanwhile, reports that Brenda is still catatonic but went ballistic when she heard the word Buffalo.

Catherine questions Tina again about her clothes, and the fact that there was no blood on them. She reminds Tina that she'd said she hugged her mother's body, and tripped over her father's body on the way out. Tina stands firm that she is telling the truth. Grissom says that the evidence tells a different story.

Nick and Brass interview the guys who own the scooter, one of them, Jesse Overton, admits that he had a sexual relationship with Tina. While they talk to him, he pulls out a cigarette that matches the butt that Nick found at the scene. Nick tells him that there's no smoking in the interview rooms, and takes the cigarettes and then asks for the matches too. They get a warrant to search Jesse's house, and find bloody clothes in the garbage.

They question Jesse Overton. He says that Tina let him in and let him choose which knife to use. When asked if the reason for committing the murders, he says that it was because Tina's parents wouldn't let them see each other. Throughout his admission, the lie detector test corroborates that he's telling the truth on everything but his motive.

Grissom, wanting to understand the motive behind the homicide, Grissom goes over the personal effects taken from the scene, and finds a necklace with a buffalo on it. He phones Sara at the hospital to find out if Brenda was a victim of sexual assault, and Sara takes UV photographs of her.

Catherine, engrossed in her assignment to map the interior, notices something that had been overlooked. They show that the father wasn't running towards Brenda's room, he was coming out of Brenda's room when he was killed. This means that the father was killed first, and the mother was killed second.

Sara shows the pictures of Brenda to Tina; they show extensive bruising. Tina admits that she knew her little sister was being sexually assaulted by their father. She says that her mother and brothers should have protected her from her father, and that he sexually assaulted her when she was young. She goes on to say that Brenda was her daughter, AND her sister, and she couldn't stand the thought of Brenda going through what she had gone through.

Sara and Brenda sit in the hospital; Sara takes her hand and Brenda smiles for the first time.

Memorable Quotes

Grissom: What did you find out about the psych exam on the little girl?

Sara: The shrink says the kid is in a catatonic state from a trauma. I

could've told you that. But she did respond to the name "Buffalo."

Grissom: Respond how?

Sara: She freaked out.

Catherine: That would be Grissom.

Eddie: How is your boyfriend?

Catherine: Ed.

Warrick: You need to tell somebody when you're cutting the lights.

Grissom: What, are you working for OSHA now?

Grissom: Hey, stop! Evidence!

Det. O'Riley: We got to hug the wall? This is the only room with no blood in it. There's nothing to disturb.

Grissom: You guys will never get it, will you?

Grissom: What's wrong with your two guys?

Det O'Reilly: They've been inside.

Ecklie: I just got off the phone with the Sheriff. He wants results, Gil.

Grissom: He should go to a sports book. I hear the Stardust is good.

Ecklie: No. What he should do is go to his first team... my team.

Grissom: Teams, Conrad? I didn't know this was a competition.

Ecklie: Well, it is, and my crew usually wins.

Grissom: Really? Didn't graveyard beat day shift in softball last summer?

Ecklie: You know, you can joke all you want. It's your ass on the line.

Grissom: I think it was 14-3.

Ecklie: Like I said, it's all about results. And, if you don't get them, I will.

Sara (looking at Brenda's coloring): That's very pretty.

(Brenda scratches out the picture.)

Sara: Or not.

Sara: Want to go for another ride?

Sara: I'll take that as a "yes."

Grissom: Do you feel this?

Sara (nods): Her soul's still in the room.

Gil: Yet who would've thought the old man could have so much blood in him?

Anonymous

This is the eighth episode of the first season of CSI Las Vegas.

Synopsis

In a fairly nondescript hotel room, a man pours himself a drink, walks into the bathroom and looks in the mirror, then hears a sound, and turns, startled. These are the final moments of the man's life.

Grissom arrives at the hotel room, and Brass takes him into the bathroom. The man is in the tub, swaddled in a sleeping bag, the window left open. Grissom says the scene is exactly like that of Royce Harmon's murder. asks if the suicide note is in the same place, and pulls a small tape recorder out of the corpse's hand but it's playing backwards. When played in the right direction, a voice identifies himself as Stewart Rampler, gives his address and says that he's going to kill himself. Grissom has the recorder dusted for prints. When Sara arrives, he tells her that this case is almost exactly like the Royce Harmon case to the T: there even are false prints at the scene which lead them to Paul Milander, the man who made the mould for the rubber hand used in the crime..

Nick and Warrick, meanwhile, are given the case of a reckless driver who went off a cliff. There is no driver in the car, but there is a passenger in the back seat. A cold beer bottle near the car indicates that it may be a DUI.

Dr. Robbins tells Grissom that while there are similarities to the Harmon case, there's one difference: Rampler fought his attacker. Harmon didn't.

Nick and Warrick, after examining the scene, figure that the car was going 70 or 80 mph when it went off the cliff. They also find a set of footprints and Nick theorizes that the phantom driver ran from the car after having an accident, leaving the car perched precariously on the edge with the victim in the back seat. Warrick disagrees. He says that there was a second car, and Nick says that if there was, the second car picked up the driver. Warrick says it's a crime; Nick says it's an accident.

Sara learns Rampler's house was being fumigated and that's why he was in a hotel. He had taken his mail with him, and Sara goes through it. One of the envelopes has an upside down stamp on it. She dusts the bathroom, and finds that there are no prints—the scene has been wiped clean.

This time, the voice on the tape is the voice of the second victim, so Grissom calls Mrs. Harmon and asks if she has any recordings of her son's voice. She'd already told them that it wasn't his voice on the tape left at his murder scene, but gives them a talking frame that her son gave her last year for Mother's Day so they have an example of him talking.

Nick and Warrick talk to the doctor about the victim's injuries. He's sedated, and it will be 12 to 24 hours before he wakes up. Warrick notes that the guy has an empty wallet and is missing his watch and wedding band, supporting his theory that a crime took place.

Greg compares Rampler's DNA to the stamps and tells Sara that the piece of outgoing mail with the upside down stamp was licked by someone else.

Nick checks the car, Warrick says that there's no phantom driver at any of the hospitals. The car was rented to Walter Bangler, who Nick figures was in Las Vegas on vacation. They check the car, and there's fingerprints on the steering wheel.

Catherine and Grissom examine the Harmon suicide tape further. They discover that it is his voice on tape, but there is a noise in the background that they'd missed before: Grissom says that the noise is the rustling of paper for a suicide script.

The lab tech tells Warrick and Nick that she found specks of blue dust in the driver's prints, but can't identify what it is.

Sara finds out that Harmon and Rampler have the same birthday, but one year apart; August 17, 1958, and 1957. Grissom has a feeling that the killer is trying to communicate a specific message with the upside down stamp and the tape playing backwards. He wonders if the message is that things are going backwards, and asks Sara to see if anything even remotely relevant happened on either of those two dates. The finger print comes back as two prints overlapped; the first one is from Paul Milander, which Grissom expected. The second belongs to Grissom. Catherine points out that someone could have taken one of his discarded gloves, or gotten his finger print off a glass in a restaurant. Grissom again thinks the killer is sending a message: the message is that he (or she) has Grissom under his thumb.

Nick and Warrick raise the bet to 300 dollars-Nick still thinks that it's a simple drunk driving case but Warrick thinks a crime took place. Warrick says that he really thinks that the guy was robbed, but Nick points out that robber wouldn't let the victim buckle up safely in the back before trying to kill him.

Grissom goes to Paul Milander's warehouse workshop to talk to him. Grissom asks about the rubber hand that was used in the crime scenes, and wants to see any records of sales to distributors, but Milander says that he doesn't really keep records like that, although he appears amicable and willing to help.

After spending hours looking through books of shoe prints, Warrick finds a match; Converse size 11. Obviously Warrick hasn't spent much time in Silverlake or Austin or he would have figured out the print source in about ten seconds. The tires match a Bentley, and there are only three in Vegas, and one, in fact, was reported stolen the week before. Brass tells them that the stolen Bentley was found, but it's been completely cleaned.

Brass tells Grissom that Rampler has somehow been making cash withdrawals after his death. Grissom requests that the entire ATM machine brought in to the lab and that he be provided with pictures from any security cameras.

Nick goes over Mr. Bangler's clothes, and learns that the blue dust is pool cue chalk. Nick theorizes that Bangler was playing pool and drinking with the phantom driver, they had an accident, and the phantom driver ran away and left the car teetering on the edge of the cliff. Warrick, however, has a different opinion. He says that yes, he was playing pool, but then he left the pool hall by himself. He was then flagged down by the guy in the Bentley who flagged him down and robbed him, and then pushed the car over the edge.

Grissom, Sara and Catherine watch the series of pictures from the ATM. They feature a homeless man holding up a series of pictures of a dove that he just keeps flipping through. They speculate that the dove represents peace, and Catherine opines that it may even represent peace of mind: that justice is required for peace of mind. Grissom sums it all up: "I'm going to keep doing this over and over again until I get justice."

Nick and Warrick finally are able to talk to the victim when he comes to. Mr. Bangler explains that he wasn't robbed, and no one did this to him. He tells them that he was drunk and shouldn't have been driving. He was playing pool and lost, but didn't have money to pay up, and so he was beaten up and robbed of his ring, wallet, and watch. When he drove home, he was drinking and swerved to avoid a truck, and went over the edge of the embankment, but had enough time to get into the back seat and buckle up before the car fell. They agree that their bet is a draw.

After an exhaustive search, the homeless man is found and Grissom talks to him. Grissom asks the bum about the man who paid him to flip the pictures; the bum says that the guy offered him 100 dollars to flip the cards. He was about 5'10" with jet black hair, blue eyes, and a bad complexion, and spoke with a stutter. He realizes that the culprit is Milander.

Sara finds an article about two hotel security guards that exonerated in the killing of a Mr. Milander, and that Paul Milander watched from the closet while the guards put his father in the bathtub and shot him, making it look like a suicide. The crime happened on August 17, 1959.

The police locate Milander's warehouse and enter, but it's almost completely empty. The lone object: stool in the middle of the floor, with an envelope on it that has "Grissom" written on it. It contains nothing but a blank sheet of paper. Grissom says, "We have nothing."

At the station, Milander asks the receptionist if Grissom's in; she says he's out on a call. Milander tells her to tell Grissom that a friend stopped by, adding that he'll know who it was. As he walks out, he stops at the security camera and waves.

Memorable Quotes

Catherine: Blank. What's that mean?
Grissom: We have nothing.

Brass: Dr. Livingston. Your dead man is making cash withdrawals.
Grissom: Which one? The first victim or the second?
Brass: The second. Stuart Rampler. The bank called. His ATM card showed a couple of withdrawals after his time of death.
Grissom: ATM machines take photographs every three seconds. Maybe we can get a Kodak moment of this guy. I want the machine here. I want prints. I want film. I want everything.
Brass: The whole machine?
Grissom: Yeah, the whole machine.
Brass: Okay.

Grissom: What happened?

Brass: You tell me Carnac.

(Grissom just caught Warrick and Nick playing video games)

Grissom: Hey! You guys want an assignment slip or a pink slip?

Warrick: Supergluing the entire car. That's a little excessive don't you think?

Nick: Hey! Man this is war.

Warrick: What's all this?

Nick: But don't drink and drive, you might spill your drink.

Nick: You care to back that up? My phantom driver against your crime scene?

Warrick: How much?

Nick: Fifty.

Warrick: I don't get out of bed for less than a bill.

Grissom: We're going off the board tonight.

Sara: Off the board?

Catherine: Old Cases. The ones that got away; fish.

Sara: Ah. I missed that one.

Stuart Rampler (Tape/recorded): My name is Stuart Rampler. I reside at 818 Noeing Hill Court, Las Vegas, Nevada. I am 43 years of age, and I'm going to kill myself. I just can't do it anymore. I love you, mom.

Grissom: You're back.

Warrick (to Nick, who's going over the victims clothes): What are you doing? His laundry?

Dr. Robbins: I've read Klausbach's report on Royce Harmon the first staged suicide.

Grissom: Similarities?

Dr. Robbins: Well, based on the entry wound, they were both murdered. But here's where it gets fun.

Catherine: That looks like he was shot trying to protect himself.

Grissom: What else, Doc? My mind is painting.

Dr. Robbins: He was paid a little visit from Mr. Muzzle stamp.

Brass: What kind of language is that? Swedish?

Grissom: It's backward.

Greg: So... what's the pot up to?

Nick: We don't bet on cases.

Greg: Ah. Of course you don't. So who's winning?

Warrick and Nick: I am.

Greg: Fiends.

Brass: Oh, you're gonna love this. Ring any bells? Rub-a-dub-dub, dead man in the tub.

Grissom: Life's like holding a dove. You hold it too hard...

Catherine: ... you kill it.

Grissom: Hold it too soft...

Sara: ... and it'll fly away.

Nick: Aww...want me to make you a bottle and go night-night?

Warrick: Aww....want me to clock your jaw and make you go night-night?

Warrick: There's other questions to answer first.

Nick: Like what?

Warrick: Footprints and tire treads.

Nick: I hate you.

Warrick: You love me. Who are you kidding?

Brass: Quincy wants to be alone.

Uniformed Cop: Why does he want to be alone?

Brass: He wants to get his mojo working.

Unfriendly Skies

This is the ninth episode of season one of CSI Las Vegas.

Synopsis

Called to investigate a beating of a first class passenger on a flight to Las Vegas, Grissom was forced to interview almost every passenger to piece together the story of what happened. Tony Candelwell appeared to be fine from his flight to Atlanta heading into Los Angeles, but on the plane to Vegas, he was labeled a bully and a psychopath by the other first class passengers.

Notable events that shaped this perception: he kicked the back seat of office worker Nate Metz, who protested because he suffered damage to his laptop as a result. Businessman Lou Everett was so busy observing the commotion that he spilled whiskey on his suit. After Metz threw his laptop at Candelwell, Candelwell mocked him and Everett was going to punch him for being obnoxious and for making him spill more of his drink. He missed by a mile and Candelwell used a CD-ROM from Metz's computer to cut Lou's face.

Max Valdez didn't want to get involved, but his wife Marlene made him and he was pushed by Candelwell into the serving cart. Marlene then tried to cut Candelwell and got his hand. Candelwell, with his hand bleeding, tried to use the bathroom but it was locked while passengers Vicki Mercer and Carl Finn were inside joining the "Mile High club".

Candelwell then mistakenly tried to open the cockpit door, and then the door to the plane itself. Preston Cash was legally blind but heard Max and Lou jumping Candelwell at the exit. To escape the fray he'd caused, Candelwell crawled towards coach, but was stopped by Max, Lou, Marlene, Nate and Dr. Keira Buerhle.

After the intense beating by the mob that had formed, Candelwell died. The doctor tried to perform CPR but to no avail. Grissom concluded from his interviews that Dr. Buerhle, Nate Metz, Lou Everett and the Valdezes were guilty of murder, but the Sheriff decided they were acting out of self defense and understandable panic, and didn't charge them.

Candelwell's bullying behavior was determined by the CSI Laboratories to be a result of enlarged cranial encephalitis, caused by the high altitude and cabin pressure. It took 5 people to kill Candelwell. It would've taken 1 person to save his life.

Memorable Quotes

Sheriff Mobley: You've got a whale of an opportunity here, Gil. A dead body on an airplane. The FAA has jurisdiction, but the Feds won't be here till sunrise. That gives us 12 hours to be heroes.

Grissom: I don't follow you.

Sheriff Mobley: Well, we either hand over the guy who did it when the Feds get here, or we give them all the glory while we watch from the sidelines.

Grissom: I don't even know if we have a homicide yet.

Grissom: ...I need their shoes.

Catherine: Why you telling me?

Grissom: Because you're the "people" person, right?

Catherine: Well, why don't you tell them that? They're not giving me bupkus.

Grissom: Please?

Catherine: Okay, people. Listen up. Shoes...off. Now.

Sara: I take it that's not blood?

Grissom: No, but it has protein in it.

Sara: Ah, the mile high club. That means the two passengers may have had no idea what was going on inside that cabin.

Grissom: High altitude enhances the entire sexual experience. It increases the euphoria.

Sara: Well, it's good. I don't know if it's that good...Cite your source.

Grissom: Would you hand me a swab please?

Sara: You're avoiding the question. "Enhances sexual experience. Increases euphoria." Cite your source.

Grissom: A magazine.

Sara: What magazine?

Grissom: "Applied psychodynamics in forensic science".

Sara: Never heard of it.

Grissom: I'll get you a subscription.

(Sara doesn't say anything)

Grissom: Now cite your source.

Sara: Oh, now you wanna go down that route?

Grissom: Yeah.

Sara (Smiles and shakes her head): Nah, nevermind.

Grissom: You started it.

Sara: Delta Airlines, Flight 1109, Boston-Miami, March '93, Ken Fuller. Hazel eyes, Organic Chem Lab TA, BMOC...overrated...in...every aspect. (Grissom looks at her) Could we get back to work please?

Grissom: Yeah, I think due to your uh...first hand knowledge and experience in airplane bathrooms you should do the swab

Grissom: Mr. Cash, you got to help me. I got eight eyewitnesses with various stories. I put them all in a mixing bowl, add eggs, milk, stick it in the oven, and all I got is a limp soufflé

Grissom: If nothing criminal happened on that flight... why isn't anybody talking to us?
Catherine: I'm going to go out on a limb here... and say... they're hiding something?
Grissom: Then we get to play hide-and-seek

Sheriff Mobley: Arrest would be good for you. It would be good for me, too. Good for Las Vegas.
Grissom: You running for mayor

Grissom:: If just one person had stopped and taken the time to look at the guy, to listen to him, to figure out what was wrong with him it might not have happened. It took five people to kill him. It would have only taken one person to save his life

Grissom: A, B, C, D or all of the above? Standoff with the police -- guy gets shot in the chest, runs back into his burning house inhaling smoke as he goes. The roof collapses, the air conditioning unit falls on his head, he dies. What killed him?

Grissom: I want this whole plane taped off ... nose to tail and wing to wing.

Brass: Oh, it's going to take a lot of tape.

Grissom: I've got a dead body, a crime scene with wings. Something very wrong happened in this plane

Sex, Lies, and Larvae

This is the tenth episode of the first season of CSI Las Vegas.

Synopsis

In the woods, a couple finds a bug-infested body, and call LVPD.

Grissom and Sara arrive on the scene to investigate. Brass tells them that it looks like the victim was shot in the head, and no weapon has been found. Grissom takes some coffee from an officer and pours it into a jar with the paper moth maggots he's collected from the body, and collects four beetles, which he predictably names Ringo, John, George, and Paul. Sara notes that the woman wasn't killed there, but was just dumped there, perhaps by someone who felt too rushed to bury her.

While Grissom and Sara are working on the body found in the woods, Catherine and Warrick are to look into a possible abduction of a Paul Sorenson, called in by a Mr. Ziegler; Nick gets a missing person named Sheryl Applegate, reported by her husband after she took the car to drive to L.A., but never arrived there. Because the car was found at the bus station, Nick dismisses the case quickly, saying the woman took the bus, duh, but he is admonished and instructed to treat it as a crime until he is sure.

Catherine and Warrick go to Mr. Ziegler's house, and on the way, Warrick tells her that child protective services called to question him about Catherine's prowess as a mother. She explains that her ex husband called CPS on her after she was late from work to pick up their daughter, but is still shocked and embarrassed. When they arrive, Mr. Ziegler answers the door and shows them a wall. The missing person was actually a painting—a Paul Sorenson painting. Mr. Ziegler tells he noticed it gone and heard a noise, perhaps the thief sneaking out. The door was open, and the security alarm was disengaged. Both Warrick and Catherine decide that it must be an inside job.

Meanwhile, Sara notes that the shot that killed the victim was fired at close range. Dr. Robbins tells them that x-rays show that she has facial fractures that suggest long-term domestic abuse. The team is no closer to finding out who she is or where she is from, however, until Grissom finds a Muscat fly on the woman's body, which only come from urban areas.

At the site of the stolen painting, Warrick finds a clue. On the wall, there is a print of an ear. This could indicate that the thief pressed his head to the wall to see if the picture was wired.

Finally, there is a break in the case of the body found in the woods: Brass says the woman has been identified as Kaye Shelton, who lived downtown in the Fremont area, and was married to Scott Shelton. He also notes that the neighbors heard a gun shot five days ago. Immediately, they hightail it downtown to interview Scott Shelton. He says that he was out of town, and when he came back she was gone, and that the gun shot heard by the neighbor could have been a TV. Grissom presses Scott about the facial fractures. He claims that he never smacked her around.

On the Strip, Nick investigates the car of the allegedly missing woman who never turned up in LA. Nick finds some hair in the car, which matches the hair color of the missing woman, and has the car towed to the lab.

At the Ziegler house, Catherine prints the whole family to compare the prints to the one from the wall. There's a match to the print from one of the sons, Jason Catherine asks where the painting is, and Jason doesn't immediately volunteer the answer, waiting until Catherine tells him that he'll be arrested if it's disappeared, regardless of his father's wishes. He admits to them that the painting is in his car.

At Mr. Shelton's house, Sara, Grissom, and Brass look around. Brass finds a gun that has recently been cleaned but Shelton says he cleaned it before he left town, and that the missing bullets were fired at a shooting range. They take the remaining bullets for testing. Sara walks down the hallway and finds a fiber on the floor, and Sara sprays for blood and finds stains on the wall. Shelton says he has no idea how it got there and a shouting match ensues between Sara and him. This does little to convince the team that he didn't abuse his wife.

At the lab, Grissom concludes that Mrs. Shelton has been dead for three days, not five, and that means that Mr. Shelton couldn't have done it if indeed he was out of town.

Catherine, meanwhile, informs Warrick that the painting taken out of Jason's car was a fake. The painting stolen was not. They decide to check Jason's dorm room for the original.

Nick vacuums the car and finds no more hair, no signs of foul play, and notes that it's too clean, but spraying for blood yields results. Finally, he agrees that this is indeed a homicide, not a case of a woman who chose to take the bus instead of her car.

Grissom, determined to crack the case, goes back to the evidence room to check the blanket that the body was wrapped in. He theorizes that the body may have been wrapped in the blanket tightly enough that insects took longer to get in and lay their eggs. He had determined, based on his knowledge of the insects infesting the body and their life cycles that the body had been cold for three days. But if his theory is correct, and the blanket was indeed that tight, she may have died five days before being discovered.

Nick learns that one of the missing woman's credit cards at the Four Aces Motel, which is near where her car was found. He takes uniformed officers with him and locates the room purchased with her credit card. When they break down the door, they find Mrs. Appleton handcuffed to the bed, and a man in the other room. Despite what it looks, she insists she has not been abducted. Thee blood in her car is from an injured dog that she took to the vet's. Nick tells her that it is his responsibility to tell her husband that she has not, indeed been the victim of foul play, but that he doesn't see any need to fill in the details of where she's been and what she's been doing.

Grissom takes his evidence to the DA to see if he has a case, but the DA tells him that since his arresting officer can barely understand the evidence, he doubts that a jury will, and wants them to either give up, or find something stronger to connect Mr. Shelton to the crime.

At the Ziegler house, Mr. Ziegler is dismayed to learn that his 10 million dollar painting is a fraud. Warrick tells him that the police recovered the originals from Jason's dorm room, and that Jason's college buddies were helping him in making the fakes. After a heated argument with his son in which his son accuses him of neglecting him for his art and money, Mr. Ziegler tells Catherine that he wants to press charges.

Back at the morgue in hopes of finding something that had been overlooked, Grissom notices a blue mark on the late Mrs. Shelton's temple that they didn't see before because it was obscured by dust. It's embedded beneath the surface and won't wash away, either. Sara finds Teflon in the bullets they took from Mr. Shelton that links him to the blue spots on his dead wife's head. Scott Shelton is then arrested.

Memorable Quotes

Sara (To Grissom): I heard you were going into an autopsy. How can you just move on to another case? They're laughing at us. You know that, right? They think we're a couple of 'science nerds'. They threw out our findings.

Sara: Any idea how long she's been dead?

Doc Robbins: The elements really got to her. Grissom and his insects are going to have to figure that one out.

Doc Robbins: Have we lost you, Grissom?

Grissom: (muttering) "The worms go in the worms go out the worms play pinochle on your snout."

Sara: Shakespeare again?

Grissom: An old nursery rhyme.

Doc Robbins: A very special insect, Dr. Seuss?

Catherine: Hey, how's the body with the bugs?

Grissom: How do you know about that already?

Sara: Hey, don't look at me.

Nick: We, uh, played a hunch; checked with homicide. You were late.

Sara: I hate bees.

Grissom: Just paper wasps. They're having too much fun to worry about us.

Sara: I never get used to this part, you know when the bugs get going.

Grissom: Just doing what god intended, recycling us back to the earth.

Brass: I ID'd her body through AFIS, and located her husband.

Grissom: Let me guess. Downtown? The Fremont District?

Brass: You know, I'm not even going to ask.

Nick: Hey.

Warrick: Hey.

Catherine: Nicky, how's it going?

Warrick: What's up?

Nick: Good, good. (He looks at the painting) Are you putting one of Lindsey's drawings into evidence?

Catherine: If only her artwork brought in this kind of dough I wouldn't need to worry about her college tuition.

Nick: Yeah, I heard your missing person was a "painting".

Warrick: At least we solved our case.

Nick: Oh!

Catherine: Keep walking.

Scott Shelton: You have your hands full with her.

Grissom: So do you.

Sara: We're going to investigate your apartment. Do we need a warrant or are you going to play nice?

Scott Shelton: Come on over. I've got nothing to hide.

Sara: We'll be the judge of that.

Richard Zeigler: Well, this is, uh where the Sorenson was displayed.

Catherine: Sorenson is a painting.

Richard Zeigler: Paul Sorenson was an artist. Early 1900s.

Catherine: How dumb are we?

Warrick: What's he know about the forensic analysis of a friction ridge?

Catherine: Right on.

Grissom (To Ecklie): Then you must feel very small today by association.

Catherine: It's like a fingerprint, for your ear.

Grisson: No, Sara's gonna work with me. You've got a missing person, Sheryl Applegate. Her husband notified the police that she took the car and headed to LA, but she never showed up. A few hours ago, the PD found her car at the bus station. They requested a CSI.

Nick: She took the bus instead, case solved.

Grissom: You've still got to convince a jury.

Sara: On guns. It's got to be better than bugs. Less Latin.

Sara: You're the one who said one piece of evidence is better than ten eyewitnesses.

Grissom: What do you tape everything I say?

Scott Shelton: (after Sara discovers blood that has been wiped clean off the wall) I have no idea how it got there.

Sara: Oh...How it "got there" was when you shot your wife in the head, wrapped her in a blanket and left her on the side of a mountains!

Scott Shelton: Get that finger out of my face, bitch!

(He pushes her finger away, and she pushes him back)

Grissom: Sara!

Sara: You touch me again, you draw back a stump!

Scott Shelton: Look at her.

Grissom: Sara!

Scott Shelton: Can't you control her?

Grissom: Get him out of here, Jim!

Scott Shelton: Told you she was a handful.

Sara: Oh, you don't know a handful!

Grissom: Hey, Sara, what's the matter with you?

Sara: I am a woman, and I have a gun and look how he treated me! I can only imagine how he treated his wife!

Grissom: You have empathy for her, Sara. You want someone to pay for what was done to her. That's normal.

Sara: You want to sleep with me?

Grissom: Did you just say what I think you did?

Sara: That way, when I wake up in cold sweat under the blanket, hearing Kaye's screams ... You can tell me it's nothing. It's just empathy.

Brass: So, you planning a little late-night luau? Roast pig?

Grissom: It's an experiment. Maybe Kaye was dead five days.

Brass: I thought your bugs never made mistakes.

Grissom: They don't. People do. The victim was wrapped in a blanket. Normally a blanket or clothing doesn't impact insect maturation. The insects usually fight their way in anyway. But I examined the folds in Kaye's blanket. She was wrapped tight---maybe tighter than I realized---which would have decreased the corpse's exposure to insects

Brass: So it took longer for the insects to get in there?

Grissom: And deposit their eggs. Maybe two whole days. I've wrapped porky here pretty tight.

Brass: Well, let me ask you this. You killed a pig just for this?

Grissom: This poor ham was already on its way to someone's Christmas dinner
table.

Brass: Wouldn't a rabbit be easier?

Grissom: Gotta be a pig. Interestingly, they're the most like humans.

Brass: Yeah, I've been saying that since I was a rookie. You're on your own, pal.

The I-15 Murders

This is the 11th episode of the first season of CSI Las Vegas.

Synopsis

Grissom arrives at a supermarket to learn that Margaret Shorey went shopping and never came home. Her purse is still in the cart, but the wallet is missing. Grissom and Brass note that she dropped a jar of mustard, which broke, and surmise that she may have used the bathroom to wash her hands or dab mustard from her clothes. On the stall door is written an ominous message: "I've killed 5 women. Catch me if you can?"

Grissom hands out assignments at the lab. he gives Sara a dead body; Nick a fight at the Bellagio; and Catherine is paired Grissom on the missing woman case. Before sending everyone on their way, Grissom shows Warrick a surveillance video of him at the Monaco and the day he was supposed to be in court. Warrick admits he was at the casino but says that he wasn't gambling.

Sara and speaks to the brother of the deceased, Kenny Berlin. He says that he walked in, saw his brother dead and bleeding, and the disarray in the room, and assumed that his brother interrupted a burglary and got shot. Sara quickly looks around the apartment and notes that it contains thousands of dollars worth of computer equipment, and that the so-called burglar was using a bed sheet to collect items to steal.

Nick arrives at the Bellagio and talks to Kristy Hopkins, who tells him that the security guard grabbed her and spit on her unprovoked. The security guard disagrees, and Nick tells Kristy that he'll need her shirt.

At the Berlin house, Sara finds no blood spatters on Kenny's clothes but she does notice glass fragments in his pant cuff. She takes his clothes as evidence, and the broken window.

A handwriting analyst tells Grissom and Catherine that the person who graffiti'd the grocery store door was a lefty of low social class, and probably a woman.

After returning from the Berlin house, Sara, angry with Warrick for gambling on the clock, tells Grissom to take him off the Berlin case; Grissom believes that Warrick wasn't gambling at the Monaco and refuses to honor her request. Catherine, meanwhile, has found five bathroom stall doors, from Victorville, Salt Lake City, San

Bernardino, Mesquite and Las Vegas, all along the I-15, and all from supermarket rest rooms, with the same graffiti. She tells Grissom that although graffiti was found in supermarket bathrooms, there was no evidence to show that the women were killed in the supermarkets.

Sara talks to Kenny about the glass, and he says that his car was broken into last week, and he was wearing the same pants, but she explains that the glass shards match the fragments from the broken window. .He repeats the story of finding his brother's body, and adds that he heard a noise and walked to the window, and that must be how he got the glass in his pants.

Grissom and Catherine go to Moapa, where there's a body on the side of the I-15. The coroner tells them that this is the victim from San Bernardino, and that the decomposition on the body is very unusual, reversed from how it should be, even, as her organs are in better shape than her skin. The coroner says she was frozen Grissom concludes that they should look for a refrigerated truck. Catherine soon finds a truck that was seen along I-15 and has a female driver.

Warrick and Sara talk to Kenny again and tell him that was not broken from the outside, it was broken from the inside.

Sara asks what he used to break the window; he says he didn't, and requests a lawyer. Sara and Warrick choose not to arrest him at that time, citing a lack of evidence, and leave.

Grissom talks to Nick about Kristy, who, as it turns out is not only a friend of Nick's, but also a prostitute. Nick insists he's not sleeping with Kristy; she was pushed around and spit on by the security guard, and Nick just wants to help her. Then, needing a saliva sample from the guard to see if he indeed spit on Kristy, Nick goes to the Bellagio. He instructs the guard to write out his statement, and then put it in the envelope and seal it, and Nick will turn it over to the DA. The security guard complies.

Brass, Grissom, and Catherine ask the female trucker for a handwriting sample, and it turns out that she is left handed. Catherine faxes the writing to the analyst who compares it to the door writing and calls back with the news that they do not match. Grissom finds this unsurprising since 97% of serial killers are men. Catherine, however, observes that their female trucker is traveling with her boyfriend, so male truckers may travel with girlfriends. Perhaps a male trucker somehow manipulated his girlfriend into assisting him in some way.

Nick then talks to Kristy . She asks about the charges, and he tells her that the DA threw out the case against her for assault after learning that the security guard had indeed spit on her.

Sara and Warrick go back to the Berlin house to see if there is anything in the computer that would help them build a case. Warrick opens the casing on the tower and they find the gun in it. A little testing tells them that Kenny used the butt of the gun to break the window. They also find a motive—with Kenny's brother dead, he is the executor of his parents' estate.

Grissom and Catherine talk to the truck dispatch center and find one that was on I-15 at approximately the right time to have committed the murders. LVPD surrounds the truck, and arrest the man and the woman driving it. Indeed, in the back, they find three bodies in a freezer unit, but none of them are Margaret. Grissom theorizes that the trucker's girlfriend would lure woman out of the supermarket with a story of locking her needing help getting into her locked car so the trucker could nab her. The girlfriend would then write the graffiti on the bathroom. The woman tells them that he made her do it, and that Margaret is in the cab of the truck. There is a lock on a compartment under the bed. Margaret is inside, bound and gagged, but still alive.

At the lab, Warrick tells Sara that he was not gambling, and in fact, the tape does not show him gambling. He adds that the next time she has any interest in where he is and what he is doing on company time, she should talk to him instead of going behind his back.

Memorable Quotes

Brass: Oh, that's sanitary.

Sara: Grissom reinstated you.

Warrick: And you have a problem with that.

Sara: Let me guess. Grissom gets you to dime yourself off and now you both

feel better? You're supposed to be in court. Instead, you're placing bets for

a cheap thrill to satisfy nothing.

Warrick: Hey! This has nothing to do with you. So are we going to work

together...or not?

Sara: I'm already working.

Warrick: What's that?

Grissom: You...at the Monaco casino.

Warrick: What? I don't believe this. Now you're pulling up film on me?

Grissom: Casinos tape everyone who walks through their door, Warrick, you know that. I thought we had a deal.

Warrick: We do.

Grissom: Look, what you do on your time is nobody's business. What you do on my time is my business.

(Warrick sighs and sits down)

Warrick: I was at the casino. But I wasn't gambling.

(Grissom sits and listens to what he has to say, screen cuts to a different scene)

Grissom (reading): "I've killed 5 women... catch me if you can."

Grissom: Sara Sidle. 419.

(Grissom hands the assignment sheet to Sara)

Sara: Dead body-- bonus.

Catherine: Whoa, somebody likes their job.

Grissom: Nick Stokes-- 416, fight at the Bellagio. She says she's a friend of yours

Catherine: Ex-girlfriend, Nick?

Nick: Well, that depends. Was she the assaulter or the assaultee?

Sara: You tell us, you like leather or lace?

Nick (chuckles): No, I'm not even going there. (turns to leave, but turns back) Lace! (Sara smiles)

Grissom (about a frozen body): And she's stiff... like a two-minute burrito that's only been nuked for a minute.

Brass: A kid from a crime lab doing favors for a hooker can't make the unit look too good, huh, boss?

Grissom: Yeah, well, I'll get into it.

Brass: I bet that's just what Nicky said.

(Catherine walks past them and toward the crime scene)

Catherine: You two ladies done talking? It's hot out here.

Nick: I need your shirt.

Kristy: Why is it every time we meet you're wanting me to take my clothes off?

Nick: Because every time we meet you put yourself in a position where you have to take them off.

Grissom: That's my Big Mouth Billy Bass. It's better than a watch dog. I got some valuable stuff in here.

Nick: Yeah, I'm sure lots of people would want to steal your two headed scorpion and Miss Piggy.

Greg (about Kristy's shirt): Now, I've done this procedure on jeans and leather jackets but never on something like this. It's very see through. Very Jennifer Lopez.

Nick: Down boy.

Greg: It's going to be a tough one to prove. This is only step one. You see, when a person talks saliva naturally comes out of their mouth. Let's say that we're tossing the hog back and forth, right? What can you tell me about the hottie that goes inside this blouse, huh? Is it true she's a friend of yours?

Nick: What, is it on the internet? Might as well be. Just remember that.

Greg: My saliva is getting on you, your saliva is getting on me.

Nick: Gross.

Nick: What's that stuff?

Greg: Starch and iodine. If this is saliva, we're going to get the old Dalmatian effect. So, Nick, uh, if I wanted to meet this friend of yours ... ?

Nick: No.

Greg: Figured. That's a pretty big spot. That's more than just a spray. In fact, looks like a distinct glob of spit.

Nick: Then Kristy was telling the truth. But it doesn't mean it was the security guard's spit.

Greg: Step three.

Nick: I'm going to need a sample.

Greg: Well, the guy knows he did it. He's not going to cough it up.

Nick: If you saw the girl that went with this blouse...you'd try.

Warrick: You just don't give up.

Sara: It's a flaw.

Sara: You weren't in your office.

Grissom: And good morning to you Miss Sidle.

Catherine: You know how you're always pushing that Holy Trinity stuff?

Grissom: Father, son and Holy Ghost?

Catherine: Victim, suspect and crime scene.

Grissom: Oh, that one.

Fahrenheit 932

This is the twelfth episode of the first season of CSI Las Vegas.

Synopsis

Brass and Grissom are eating lunch when a package arrives for Grissom. It's been sent from jail, and contains a video of a Frank Damon telling Grissom that he's awaiting trial for the murder of his wife and son. Brass recognizes it as an arson case from a few months ago.

The team comes into Grissom's office to find out what they are to be working on: a dead man found in the front seat of his car is given to Nick and Catherine and Warrick and Sara are with Grissom. Catherine comments that Ecklie worked the CSI on the arson case, and Brass tells Grissom that eye-witnesses saw Damon running from the burning house, and his wife was maxed out on her credit cards. There was also gasoline found in the master bedroom and Damon bought a gallon of gas a week before the fire. So far, there is no evidence, compelling or otherwise, exonerating Damon.

In a parking garage, Nick and Catherine examine the body of the young man killed with a shot to the head. Catherine finds his empty wallet and theorizes that the killer was in the back seat, waiting for him. Nick finds something in the victim's ear, and thinks it's a hearing aid. There's condensation on the rear window, a bag on the floor of the car containing about $15,000 in cash, and a ticket saying "Giants -9," written by Teller 12. Nick and Catherine immediately seek out Teller 12, who tells them that the guy was a runner. Catherine says he was under 18 so it was illegal to have him as one. The teller says he only knows the runner's number, not his name.

At the prison, Grissom meets with Damon, who says that 6 specialists have turned him down. He elaborates on the fire: at midnight, he went out for ice cream, as his 8-year old son couldn't sleep. Twenty minutes later he returned and saw smoke coming out of the back of the house. As a volunteer firefighter, he knew that 932 degrees Fahrenheit, the smoke will flash into fire. He left the house and called in the fire from his car. Grissom mentions the gas found on the floor of the closet; Damon says he bought it for the lawnmower, and kept it in the garage; and someone else put the gas in the closet. He puts his hand up on the glass and Grissom sees it's burnt.

Despite feeling that Damon is lying, Grissom goes to the house with Warrick and Sara. They find a mattress in the living room, and a backpack with camping things in it, including waterproof matches, which Sara tags as evidence. Grissom says that the fire was contained in the bedroom, but the outside of the door frame is burned, although the door itself isn't burnt through. Ecklie reported that the point of origin for the fire was the bedroom closet. Grissom finds the point of origin, marked as narrow V-pattern on the wall, which indicates that it was a high-temperature, rapid fire. He finds shards of glass at the apex of the V, which are melted into the concrete. He notes that an accelerant was used, but there's nothing to indicate that the accelerant was spread around, which would usually happen in an arson. So far, Warrick and Sara have both concluded that Mr. Damon is guilty.

Meanwhile, Catherine has located the mother of the young man found dead in the car, Mrs. Hillman, who identifies the body of her son. She says that Joey wasn't hearing impaired, and doesn't know why he'd have a hearing aid, then tells Catherine that Danny, her other son, got Joey into being a runner. She tells Catherine that she hasn't seen Danny in a week, or heard from him, and fears that something has happened to him as well.

Nick and Catherine, in an effort to find out about what a runner is, ask Warrick. He tells them that they make 2 grand a week but they don't know whom their boss is. The boss only is experienced as a voice, has no name, and is never seen. Nick wants to find the Voice, but Warrick says that they would probably benefit more from talking to another runner, since a runner would kill for a good route.

Grissom runs tests on the flash over point. They discover that the only way for the door frame to have burned was with oxygen, which means that Damon opened the door despite his assertion that he did not.

Grissom goes back to the prison, where Damon is talking to a woman that he identifies as his sister. Grissom says that the door was opened, and looks at Damon's hand and matches the burn to the door knob. Damon begins to cry, insisting that doesn't want anyone to know that he opened the door because he's a volunteer fireman and should have known better. Grissom points out that this places him outside the fire, but Damon says that by opening the door, he let loose a fire worse than any monster, and killed his wife and son. Grissom asks gently if he lied about starting the fire too.

In a casino, Nick and Catherine find runner #702 who used to know #517 (Joey). Catherine asks who got Joey's route, but he doesn't know, saying he only knows as much as what has been on the news, and has no new information for them.

At the site of the fire, Grissom and Warrick They move the mattress and find a heater. Grissom says it was high voltage. They check the breaker box and find an overload.

Catherine gets the test results from the condensation on the car window and finds it's nasal mucus, from someone sneezing. Mrs. Hillman arrives with her son Danny tells Catherine and Nick that he took his runner money and played blackjack and lost $30,000. He went on the run because he was scared and didn't have the money to pay it back. He didn't think about the fact that someone could harm his brother to get to him, or as payback. He has no idea who did it, but Nick says that he doesn't have to give them a name, just the frequency for the hearing aid.

Grissom looks at the electrical system more carefully. The heater overheated, and that the fire started in the wall, not on the floor. Damon, however, still can't explain why there was gas in the closet, so the charges stand.

O'Reily brings in the runners; Catherine and Nick get voluntary swab from them but none match the mucus in the car.

Grissom counts the matches from the backpack and finds that none of them were used in the fire. Sara says that the melted glass demonstrates that the fire burned at over 1000 degrees, but the water from the fire hoses washed all the evidence away, and the hydrocarbon in the closet could be something other than gasoline. They go back to the house and discover that there's a clean up crew there, carting out the evidence. Grissom immediately confronts Ecklie, since he was originally his case, and he says that he didn't send the clean-up crew. He offers Grissom coffee but Grissom smacks the pot out of his hand.

Frustrated, Grissom goes back to the prison, where he sees the woman talking to Damon again. He speaks to her as she leaves and asks about Damon's relationship with his wife and son; she says he was a wonderful father, but doesn't comment on whether or not he was a good husband. He talks to Damon, and tells him he knocked a coffee pot out of Ecklie's hand earlier because he was angry, and asks Damon if he's ever lost his temper like that. After a moment of silence, Damon tells him that he didn't leave for ice cream, he was leaving for good. He says that he and his wife argued, and she was throwing things at him as he was packing. She threw a phone, a bag, a kerosene lamp with a wick, and so he left the house so the situation could defuse a little bit. He drove around for about 20 minutes. Grissom tells Damon that the space heater caused a spark in the overload, which ignited the kerosene and started the fire.

At the casino, Nick asks teller 12 where he can find runner 702, and makes small talk. Teller 12 tells him that today is his last day. He asks if the new job is Joey's old route, then asks if he got so scared when he shot Joey that he forgot to take the money. The teller says he wants a lawyer.

At the prison, Grissom shows up to offer Damon a ride, and the woman—his alleged sister-- is there as well. Damon says that she's not his sister, she's his girlfriend, and says that he thought that when he got out, he'd feel free, but he feels... as he trails off into silence, Grissom finishes his sentence with the word, "Responsible?"

Memorable Quotes

Grissom: Do I seem like the kind of guy who skips stuff?

Warrick: Are you always this blasé about professional suicide?
Grissom: Only when I'm about to commit it. You're driving.

Brass: An innocent man. Jail's full of them.
Grissom: It only takes one.

Grissom: What are you so afraid of, Conrad? We're just a couple of science geeks. Why can't we work together?
Ecklie: No, we are public servants. We investigate cases as efficiently as we can and then we move on. We're not a clearinghouse for defendants on the eve of trial who don't like what we've turned up.
Grissom: Yes, we are.. if it's our mistake that put them there.
Ecklie: Fine. Spin your wheels.

Grissom: Listen, you guys. You're like Dodger fans. The ball games only in the seventh inning and you're already out of your seats.

Brass: What's this? An anonymous package from county lockup?

Brass: Yeah, well, hey, just a second. Wait a minute. Give an innocent bystander a chance to clear out, will you?

Grissom: What are you worried about?

Brass One minute, I'm eating tomato salad. The next ... I'm gazpacho.

(Grissom opens the package and finds a video tape inside)

Brass: With any luck it'll be the next episode of G-String Divas.

Nick (evaluating Grissom): Organization... minus one.

Warrick: He lied, what do we do now?

Grissom: We chase the lie, till it leads to the truth.

Boom

This is the thirteenth episode of the first season of CSI Las Vegas.

Synopsis

In an office building, a security guard checks people's identification. A second one greets a florist and puts the flowers on the desk, and then notices a briefcase sitting on the floor. He picks it up and it explodes.

When Grissom and Catherine arrive at the scene, Brass tells them that there is only one fatality: Jake Richards, the guard that picked up the briefcase. Catherine and Grissom examine the body, and note that both his ears were taken off, which means that he was looking directly at the bomb when it detonated. Catherine notes the point where the bomb went off and says that since the guard's clothes are burnt but not torn, it means that the bomb contained a low velocity propellant. No clues, so far, point to the identity of the assailant.

Grissom tells Catherine, Sara and Warrick that there are thousands of pieces of forensic evidence lying around, telling them how the bomb went off, and they have to find them and put them back together. Warrick takes pictures of the crowd, Sara sifts through the debris, and Catherine collects shrapnel.

Nick leaves a hotel where he had met a friend, and as he gets into his car, he sees Kristy gesturing at Nick for help while a man grabs her arm. The man leaves when Nick tells him to get lost. Nick offers to give her a ride home, and although he does just intend to drop her off, she convinces him to come inside.

At the office building, Catherine finds a cog with the letters FP engraved on it. Grissom enlists Dominic, the head of security for the building to help in the investigation. Grissom, suspecting Dominic and wanting to keep him close for observation, tells an officer to keep an eye on the guy.

The next morning, Nick calls Kristy for a late breakfast and drives to her house to meet her. When he arrives, the house has been taped off into a crime scene. They have a 419—a murder. Nick is appalled. After talking to one of the officers to see what happened, he leaves.

Dominic explains how to make a pipe bomb to Warrick and Brass in an interview room, piquing Grissom and Brass' suspicion. A public defender arrives, instructing Dominic not to say anything more, and they leave together.

Sara looks over all the bomb pieces collected from the scene and asks how the victim could avoid dismemberment, and Catherine explains that there's a vacuum created when the bomb goes off. Grissom comes in with a piece of the timing device, saying that the bomb was time-delayed.

Nick arrives, desperate to talk to Grissom. He tells him what happened—how he wasn't dating Kristy until the night before, and now she's dead. He tells Grissom that he knows what Ecklie will find in the house - his finger prints and DNA. Grissom tells him that innocent people don't give statements, and Nick should refrain from talking about what happened. He tells Nick to go for a walk, suggesting that he might see Jack—the man grabbing onto Kristy's arm the night before-- and if so, he should identify him, but not try to talk to him.

Catherine goes to the morgue and learns the Kristy died while struggling, and the murder weapon hasn't been found. The coroner hasn't printed the body and is worried that he might find Nick's prints, but Catherine tells him that if Nick's innocent, there is nothing to worry about even if the prints are on her body.

Warrick comes in to Grissom's office, where he's researching timers, and says that Catherine wants him to find the tool used to engrave the FP, and asks for guidance. Grissom tells him that he has to find the tool by a process of elimination; he then goes to the lab and checks various ways to engrave, and compares them to the FP found on the bomb piece.

Ecklie knocks on Grissom's door and says that Nick's prints were all over the house; Nick agrees to give a DNA sample with no warrant necessary. He also gives Ecklie Jack's license plate, gleaned from security footage at the hotel. Ecklie tells him he's not going to follow it up. He goes on to comment that he doesn't want to think that a CSI could commit murder, but he also wouldn't have thought that a CSI would have sex with a prostitute. Catherine intervenes as the argument is getting more and more heated, and pulls Nick away.

Grissom and Sara, having figured out that the bomb was in a briefcase, are in the desert, for to see what kind of pipe may have been used. Experiments lead them to conclude that the bomber used something like a muffler or tail pipe.

Brass tells them to check Dominic's house; Dominic has bought seven of the most popular clocks used for bombs in the recent past.

Grissom and Brass go to Dominic's house and ask him to show them the clocks he purchased. He tells them that he makes bombs all the time, and even kept a piece of the bomb that detonated at the building for "sentimental" reasons. Brass arrests him and as the officers lead him out with a jacket over his head to protect his privacy, Grissom comments that he doesn't know if Dominic is brilliant or insane. Brass says that if he's not guilty, he's putting on a great show.

In the lab, Sara tests the orange substance found at the scene of the detonation, and finds that it's polyethylene terathalate.

In the morgue, Dr. Robbins tells him that Kristy didn't have any family that they can find, and Nick, despite the fact that it may look bad, says he'll give her a proper burial.

In the holding cells, Grissom talks to Dominic and tells him that the evidence raises serious questions about his innocence, but Dominic stands by his claim that despite his enthusiasm for explosives, he wasn't responsible. As

Grissom leaves him, Brass tells him that there's been another bombing at a car rental dealership.

There manager was working and there was one fatality. Grissom finds a mousetrap, which acted to set off the timer on the bomb. Sara talks to the manager. He has on an orange jacket, which she takes as evidence because it's polyethylene terathalate, or polyester, and it's orange.

Grissom tells Dominic that he's free to go; Dominic tells Grissom that it's been a pleasure and a privilege to watch him work. Grissom tells him that he shouldn't be so trusting.

Catherine tells Brass that she ran priors on Jack, the man who Nick scared away from Kristy, and he has sexual assault conviction on his record from 1988. In an interview Jack admits that he had a fight with Kristy and was going to her place to apologize. When he got there, he saw her physically fighting with a guy and he took off because it wasn't his business, and he's no hero. He says that the guy was the one that he'd seen earlier on the Strip, Nick something.

Outside the room, Ecklie says that Jack sounds believable but Catherine asks for 12 hours with access to the evidence and crime scene. The Sheriff agrees to this, but tells her that after that time, they'll arrest Nick unless she comes up with a compelling reason that they shouldn't.

Catherine asks to examine the semen sample from the condom. She discovers after placing the sample under a microscope that the sperm is all head and no tails. She tells Grissom that this means that the sex took place around 2 a.m., and Kristy's time of death was around 6 a.m. Still, there is no way to prove that Nick hadn't stayed an extra four hours after they were finished.

Sara tells Grissom that the headquarters for the bombed car rental is in the building where Dominic works, and that at that office, there's a disgruntled employee named Norman Stirling.

They go to Stirling's house after doing a background check. Brass points out that they got a restraining order against him because he became violent and threw around furniture at their head office. They find orange jackets hanging in the garage, the same as the manager of the rental place was wearing., and Brass arrests him.

Catherine goes to Kristy's house to search for the murder weapon. She compares the ties on the drapes to the pictures of the marks around Kristy's neck. She takes the rope to Greg and wants him to extract DNA from epithelial on the rope, and he complies.

After the results come back, Catherine finds Nick in the lunch room. She tells him that the match was dead-on, and it proves that Jack killed Kristy.

Warrick tells Grissom that he figured out an electric etcher was used to make the FP on the bomb piece. They were bought in bulk recently from the Las Vegas school district. There is one school that used them, and Stirling's son goes to that school. Tyler says that his dad worked at the car rental place for 30 years before he was fired. Brass asks what FP is, and Tyler tells them it's 'Fair Play', and that he thinks that after 30 years, his father is entitled to it. Mr. Stirling is horrified. Tyler tells him that he learned how to make bombs on the internet to avenge his father. Grissom asks him to tell them if he's made any more, and where they are.

At Dominic's home, he listens to the police scanner and hears the bomb report at a school. He dashed out the door before he has a chance to hear that the bomb is triggered and time-delayed. He arrives at the school and runs through the halls, finding a box in the locker number that was reported on the police scanner. He picks it up and carries it outside; Grissom and other officers arrive and see him with it. Grissom pleads with him to put it down and Dominic asserts that it's safe just before it explodes.

Nick sees Jack as he is booked and wants to know why he did it, telling him that Kristy was changing her life and getting out of the business, going back to school. Jack says that she was going back to college just to recruit more girls, not to learn anything or rebuild her life. He was her pimp, and she was leaving him in order to set up her own business. Then, demonstrating his keen grasp on the obvious, he informs Nick that "this isn't Pretty Woman, she's not Julia Roberts and you're not Richard Gere."

In his office, Grissom reads the paper and tears out a clipping to put on the wall. It's an article with the headline, "Local Hero Gives Life" and is about Dominic.

Memorable Quotes

Grissom: The Van Gogh effect... in stereo. Both ears gone.

Catherine: Who? Why? Will he do it again? Only time will tell.

Brass (to Sara and Grissom, who are trying to identify the pipe used in the bombings): Don't you love the smell of sulfur in the afternoon?

Sara: Hey.

Grissom: Could you find that and turn it off, please?

Sara: Find the clock our guy used?

Grissom (sighs): Not yet.

Sara: This is a good choice. According to the bomb data center which has a record of every component used in any bomb -- from Ted Kaczynski to teenage boys playing with fireworks -- the most recent timing device of choice is made by

TimeTell SnoozeWell, $10.99 at any local drugstore.

Grissom: You spoiled all my fun.

(Grissom starts to take apart the clock and Warrick walks in)

Warrick: Gris, can I get something clear here?

Grissom: Anything's possible.

Warrick: Catherine gave me this "FP" which was part of the Hansen bomb and I'm supposed to figure out what tool the bomber used to engrave it.

Grissom: You isolate the tool, and then we trace it.

Warrick: Yeah, but he could've used any number of things to initial it. I mean, screwdriver, a drill bit, a box cutter.

Grissom: It's the same as guns-- we eliminate them one at a time.

Warrick: What are you guys doing?

Sara: We're going to go blow up some bombs.

Warrick: Oh, I definitely got the wrong end of this investigation.

Grissom: Alas, poor Warrick.

Grissom: I can't tell whether he's brilliant or nuts.

Brass: Sound familiar?

Grissom: You told me you weren't dating her.

Nick: I wasn't till last night after I broke up her fight with this guy, uh... Jack.

Grissom: And Ecklie's at her house now.

Nick: Yeah, and I can tell you what he's going to find. My fingerprints; my DNA.

Grissom: What were you thinking, Nicky?

Nick: I wasn't.

Catherine: The sperm from the condom was frozen at 10:15 am. It's all heads, no tails.

Grissom: I'm not quite up to speed about the particulars of....

Catherine: It takes about 7 hours for bacteria to eat away at the tails, that places time of ejaculation at around 2am. But Kristy's death was at around 6am.

Grissom: Well, that suggests a lag between ejaculation and Kristy's murder. But that doesn't disprove Nick's presence at the time of the homicide.

Catherine: You could be a little more supportive.

(Looking at Nick's sperm)

Greg: Nick's little soldiers.

Ecklie: I need a DNA sample from you, Nick.

Nick: I assume you're trying to prove Kristy Hopkins and I were sexually active last night.

Ecklie: We found a condom, used.

Nick: And my DNA will match, no warrant necessary. And I have something else for you. I got this off a valet surveillance tape.

Ecklie: A license plate number?

Nick: Vehicle belongs to Jack Willman. Had a fight with Kristy Hopkins outside the Orpheus last night around midnight.

Ecklie: Well, I'll look into it but come on--your fingerprints, your DNA, that's what's going into evidence.

Nick: You just love that, don't you?

Ecklie: You think I want to believe a CSI could commit murder? Hell I don't even want to believe that a CSI could sleep with a hooker.

Catherine: You know what? Nick's private life...

Ecklie: Is no longer private. Catherine, I'm sorry if you guys don't like where the evidence is pointing. But show me otherwise--tell me I'm wrong. In the meantime, my hands are tied. I have protocol to follow.

Nick: I hate that guy.

Greg: I would never doubt your word.

Catherine: Smart man.

Catherine: I think we'd better head over to the police station.

Nick: DNA didn't pan out huh?

Catherine: Never have I seen such a clean match. Jack Willman killed her.

Nick: Thank you.

Catherine: Hey, I'm just doing my job. Besides if they'd sent you to jail I'd get stuck with all your cases.

Brass: There's been another fourth of July.

Sara: He's been out of work ever since.

Grissom: Sittin' around, makin' bombs..

Catherine: Oh, these fire guys really know how to trash a crime scene.

Grissom: That's what they do. Put wet stuff on the red stuff.

To Halve and To Hold

This is the fourteenth episode of the first season of CSI Las Vegas.

Synopsis

Grissom and Catherine arrive after a dog retrieved a human bone from the desert during a game of fetch. Grissom says it's a tibia, that has been in the desert long enough to be picked clean.

Grissom, Catherine and Nick are assigned to work on the bone; Sara and Warrick get a dead 23 year old man found in the Lucky Seven motel.

In the desert, teams of officers search for more bones. They find a piece of wrist bone and a rib, flagging the sites where bones were found. Soon they end up with 100 fragments.

At the Lucky Seven, Sara and Warrick go into the room and find Darren Pyne's body in a room where there was a party. He's been hit on the head with a lamp. The room is registered to Celine Dion, but the credit card on the room belongs to Lynn Henry, from Wisconsin. Sara and Warrick go to the Venetian Hotel, where they find Lynn Henry and her friends Meg and Joyce having lunch. The news is broken to them that Darren is dead. Lynn explains that they had a bachelorette party for Meg last night; they hired a male dancer at the room at the Lucky 7. She says that Darren arrived around 10 p.m., they left at 3 a.m. and let him stay in the room. Sara asks about bruises on Lynn's wrists, she says she doesn't know how she got them because she was pretty faded for the bachelorette party.

Grissom and Catherine put the bones together to form a skeleton, and determine that the body is that of a male based on the pelvic bone, that he was about six feet tall, and he was about 60 or 70 years old, but they don't know his race. Teri Miller arrives and tells them that they can determine if he was alive or not when he was dismembered by looking for soft tissue in the bones. Grissom isn't happy that Catherine called Teri Miller and has a word with Catherine about it. Teri looks over the skeleton and rearranges a wrist bone and ankle bone, but tells Grissom that otherwise, it's well done.

Nick checks the dental society database and gets a hit for their jawbone from a local dentist, identifying the dead body as that of Mel Bennett, 70 years old. Teri examines the bones and determines that a reciprocating saw was used to cut up the body.

Dr. Robbins, meanwhile, talks to Warrick about the male dancer. Warrick says that the women admitted to lap dances, but nothing more. Dr. Robbins says that he died at around midnight. A swab shows vaginal cells which are fresh, meaning that Darren had sex just before he died. Warrick and Sara bring in the women to determine who was lying about both the sex and the time that they left. At first, they sit silently. Then Lynn admits that after they all left, she went back to the room to get her purse, and while there, Darren attacked her and forced himself on her, which explains the bruises on her wrists. She says that he was alive when she left the room the second time. The women want to leave for Meg's rehearsal dinner. Warrick and Sara let the rest go but tell Lynn that she'll be taken to a hospital for a rape kit.

Grissom, Catherine and Brass arrive at the Bennett home to speak to the widow of the man found in the desert. Mrs. Bennett answers the door. They ask to speak with her husband and she tells them that he's gone to the store. They place her in a cruiser while they examine the house. Searching the bathroom, Catherine finds no drugs, and swabbing for blood in the bathtub, finds some in the drain. Brass comes in from the garage and says he's found the saw used to cut up the body. At the lab, Teri experiments with a similar saw on a pig's bones. She tells them that the skipping marks on the bones show that the person who used it was not used to handling it, or was weak.

Warrick and Sara examine the room at the motel again. Warrick finds something on the edge of the bed that Sara identifies as a tiny diamond. Sara suggests that it might have come from the engagement ring of Meg, the bride.

In the interview room, Brass, Catherine and Grissom speak to Mrs. Bennett, asking about the saw and why she didn't report him missing after he was gone for seven months. Mrs. Bennett tells them that she wants an attorney. They have her sign a form before calling a lawyer for her, noting that her hands are so bad that she can barely use or pick up the pen.

Sara gets a page that Lynn's rape kit exam results are in, and that there is no evidence of rape. They arrive at A Little White Chapel while the wedding is in progress and arrest all the women who were at the bachelorette party for murder.

Catherine examines the tissue Teri Miller collected from the bone. Because there is no blood on it, the body was cut up post mortem. Mrs. Bennet, after another round of questioning, admits that she cut the body up, and her lawyer reminds CSI that it's not against the law in Nevada to do that. The lawyer says that Mrs. Bennett came home from shopping and found him dead in the tub. Mrs. Bennett, despite noting that her husband was dead, has been receiving and cashing her husband's checks for the last seven months. While cutting up a body is not illegal in Nevada, fraud is. Still, though it proves a motive, it doesn't prove a murder.

Greg runs tests on the marrow that show the presence of a lot of digoxin, demonstrating that Mr. Bennett was poisoned. They speak to Mrs. Bennett again in her home, and Mrs. Bennett says that her husband was in chronic pain and very ill. He wanted her to help him commit suicide, but she couldn't do it, so she left while he did it himself, instructing her to hide his body so that she could continue to receive his pension checks. Still, there is no proof, other than circumstantial evidence, that she killed him.

Sara explains to the women that injuries at certain places on the vagina indicate consent, while injuries at others indicate forced sex. Sara tells the women that Lynn showed no evidence of sex in the last 48 hours, or even in the last four months. But someone had sex with Darren. Meg admits that it was her, and it wasn't rape. She tells Sara that at first, she felt that it was ok—it was Vegas, and so it didn't really count. But then she realized that what she was doing was wrong, and tried to get Darren to stop but he wouldn't, and so she hit him with the lamp to get him to stop, not to kill him. Sara asks about Meg's rings, and she tells them that hers is a diamond but Luke's ring is a zirconium setting since they wanted to save money for the honeymoon.

They talk to Luke and observe that one of the zirconium is missing. Warrick theorizes that Luke found out about the party and showed up at the motel; that he argued with Joyce and Lynn outside, getting physical with them and even bruising Lynn's wrists. When he finally went into the room, he caught Meg having sex with Darren, he threw the lamp, and bashed Darren's head against the edge of the bed, killing him, and leaving the piece from his ring behind. The couple is handcuffed and driven off in a cruiser.

In a restaurant overlooking the Strip, Grissom and Teri are at dinner when his beeper goes off; two bodies have been found in a crack house, and they've been dead for some time. His phone rings, and he turns to take the call, giving instructions on what to do with the bodies until he arrives;

when he turns back around and puts down the phone, Teri is gone.

Memorable Quotes

Grissom: You failed to report him missing for seven months because ... ?
Rose Bennett: I don't like your tone, young man.

Sara: (Referring to a victim's vagina) It does tell a monologue.
Catherine: So, are you thinking what I'm thinking?
Grissom: How amazing the universe is. Everything made from the same carbon, stars to trees, trucks to human bones.
Catherine: Uh, no, I was thinking that we have about 100 bone fragments. We could ID this body before the end of the shift.
Grissom: Hmm.
Catherine: Stars and trucks?

Catherine: What are you doing?
Grissom: Bones are porous. They stick to the tongue (puts piece in mouth again) and this doesn't stick. (puts it back down) It's a piece of rock.
Catherine: I-I hope you had your hepatitis B shot. Did you?
Grissom: Could be a piece of wrist bone.

Catherine: Well, do you want to suck on it...to be sure?

Catherine: Well, it is a leg bone and my guess is that it didn't walk out here by itself.

Grissom: It could have been a hiker who got lost. It's interesting to me how you always expect the worst.

Catherine: You see, that way I'm never disappointed. And sometimes I'm nicely surprised.

Grissom: Potential crime scene. Did you know there are 206 bones in the human body?

Catherine: Yes professor. I, too, took osteology.

Grissom: Well, 205 more bones and we have a complete skelton. If we find the rest then we can determine if or if not it was a murder.

Catherine: Well, I feel it in everyone of my 206 bones that this was a murder.

Greg: Skeletal muscle of Mel Bennett. It goes in... contents come out. In 30 seconds.. bioassay. I like saying that word. Bioassay. Sounds nubian.

Grissom (trying to reconstruct the skeleton): "All the king's horses and all the king's men couldn't put Humpty Dumpty back together again."

Warrick: Who's the room registered to?

Sara: Well, you know, that would be Celine Dion.

Grissom: I'll take toe bones for $200, Alex.

Catherine: That is correct...according to this book.

Grissom: You bring in a specialist without my approval?
Catherine: What? And you don't bring one in, possibly compromise the case because you two had a relationship?
Grissom: Relationship? I hardly know that woman.
Catherine: Oh, so I guess that dopey look in your eye whenever she's around is just that.

Teri: (To Grissom) Well you are the bug guy.

Catherine: Are the bones whispering to you?

Grissom: What's next?
Teri Miller: Mutilation in the Everglades.
Grissom: Maybe it was just an alligator.

Brass: How'd you guys do?
Catherine: We found blood in the drain.
Grissom: You find anything?
Brass: Just the murder weapon.

Teri Miller: It's kind of like that old saying: 'How a person does one thing is...

Grissom:... how a person does everything.'

Table Stakes

This is the fifteenth episode of the first season of CSI Las Vegas.

Synopsis

At a formal party, the guests—which include a sheriff--toast the picture of Portia Richmond, the homeowner, who isn't present, and the 1.6 million dollars they've raised at this charity event. The round of self-congratulations is disrupted by a piercing scream at the discovery of a dead woman floating in the pool.

Warrick, Catherine and Nick arrive; Nick completes a sketch of the home. Soon, Warrick notices something in the bottom of the pool--it's a cuff link with the initials "C. M." on it, in turquoise and silver. He shows the cuff link to Grissom who tells him to check the guest list for C. M.s.

Grissom goes to the morgue to examine the body. She has marks around her neck, and Dr. Robbins tells Grissom that she was dead before she was in the water. Grissom notes that strangulation is usually perpetrated by men, and tells Dr. Robbins to run a rape kit. Catherine gets a call about another case and sends Warrick to look into it, then calls Sara as well.

Mr. and Mrs. Haynes are the hosts of the party as the homeowner is out of town on a cruise. They tell Brass and Grissom that they didn't know the deceased and that she wasn't on the guest list.

The dead woman is identified as Lacey Duvall, a dancer. Catherine and Grissom talk to her friend, Rachel, who tells them that Lacey was seeing this mysterious rich guy who wouldn't tell her anything about himself. Grissom looks around at the things on the counter where Lacey used to sit and picks up a music box. On the bottom is an engraving plate that says, "To Portia." the date on the inscription is March 7th, 1969.

Warrick, having received a call that another body was found, meets Detective Conroy, who tells him that there's a dead man on the walkway between the hotels. The man is in a glass elevator on the Strip, and the gun used to kill him is beside his body. Warrick notes that there's a quarter stuck to the deceased's forehead and comments that in the old days, the mob used to leave a canary with the body to indicate that the deceased 'sang' but now they leave a quarter to say 'call someone who cares.' He prints the whole elevator.

Grissom and Catherine check the music boxes at Portia's house and find that they're all engraved with a March 7th date with different years, making it unlikely that Portia gave it to Lacey since the music box appears to have sentimental value. A noise startles the team and they go upstairs and find Mr. and Mrs. Haynes in the bedroom, having sex.

At the lab, Greg tells Sara that the sexual assault kit came back, and that the system showed that the semen matched a 10 year old case involving a murdered cheerleader in Texas

Mr. and Mrs. Haynes come downstairs; Brass asks again where Portia is. Patrick Haynes tells them that Portia is on a yacht somewhere in the Mediterranean and can't be reached, and demand to know if they've done something wrong. As they talks to them, Mrs. Haynes drinks some bottled water from a straw, and Grissom takes it from her. Upstairs in the bedroom, Catherine looks in the closet realizes that no clothes seem to be missing. Funny, since if Portia was on a trip, one can assume she would have packed clothing to take with her. Grissom examines the fireplace in the bedroom and finds a tooth in the ashes at the bottom. They do need, however, a comparison DNA sample to prove it came from Portia.

Catherine, Brass, and Grissom decide that the best thing to do now is to take a tour of Liberace Museum. The guide shows them the head-dress that Portia wore when she was in the Follies Bergere in 1959. Catherine examines it and finds hairs caught in it.

Warrick has identified the dead man in the elevator Tyson Green. At the time of his death, he was carrying a money roll, a receipt for food comped by the hotel, a marker from a casino and a gambling receipt. Detective Conroy tells him that the gun has come back, registered to Bobby Morgan, with no prints on it, and there are no prints from the quarter yet. Bobby Morgan, when contacted, said his gun had been stolen, however, he hadn't reported it because he didn't want his wife to know he still had it around the house.

In the hallway outside the DNA lab, Greg tells Grissom that the tooth matches the hair from the head-dress.

At a restaurant, Catherine, Brass and Grissom inform the Haynes couple that Portia may be dead. As the Haynes get up to leave; Amanda Haynes puts her coat over the chair of the table behind hers, on top of the fur coat of the woman that's sitting there, then picks up both coats. As soon as she gets outside, she and her husband are arrested for stealing the fur coat.. Grissom tells him that they found semen in Lacey's rape kit. Patrick admits that he had sex with her before the party, and that they'd been having an affair. Catherine asks if he ever gave Lacey gifts, Patrick says that he didn't, but that Lacey had been in the house and had seen and liked the music boxes.

Nick interrupts the interrogation to tell Grissom that in the case from Texas where the cheer leader was killed, the main suspect was Chad Matthews, like the C.M. on the cuff link. The real Patrick Haynes is dead: Sara discovered during the course of her research that Patrick Haynes' Social Security Number matches that of an 8-month old infant who died years ago.

More research is done. The Austin Police have five aliases for Haynes, all of them from different places and different crimes, and moreover, that a journal has been found.
Also, Portia hasn't spent a dime since leaving for her cruise according to her credit card statement.

Warrick talks to the finger print technician who tells him that there's no results on the prints from the elevator.

Catherine tells Brass, Sara and Nick discover that someone forged Portia's signature, but that a forged signature isn't a motive for murder. Nick wonders why Patrick Haynes would give up his DNA so readily if he's really Chad Matthews; Sara comments that he might have just been betting that they didn't have anything on him.

Dr. Robbins gives Grissom the photos from the autopsy; Grissom notes that Lacey is missing a fingernail. They retrieve the missing fingernail, Grissom gives Greg the straw that he took from Amanda and has him test the DNA from that against the fingernail.

In the interview room, they talk to Patrick Haynes and tell him that he's been cleared of all charges in this case, but is being extradited to Texas for the murder of the cheer leader. They bring in Amanda Haynes and tells her he's got DNA proving that Amanda killed Lacey Duvall. He speculates that Lacey told Amanda that she knew that he was really Chad Matthews, and that she was sleeping with him, so Amanda killed her. Catherine asks where Portia Richmond is; they tell her that Portia is in Europe, on a yacht. Grissom, however, puts a glass jar on the table with piranha fish in it. The piranha are from the pond on Portia's property. He says that Patrick hit Portia in the bedroom, and then dumped her in the pond where the fish ate her, destroying the body and leaving no remains.

Warrick gives the markers to the casino boss, and tells him that Tyson Green won't be paying . Warrick walks through the casino, looking at the machines and listening to the sounds of gambling.

Memorable Quotes

Catherine: 419 at The Sphere, glass elevator. You're on it.

Warrick: This is a big case. I'm in a groove here.

Catherine: Well, groove on down to the Strip.

Warrick: Whatever happened to "You cross the tape, you go the distance"?

Catherine: I was probably saying that to get you to service my needs at the time.

Sara: What am I? Working food and beverage at one of the hotels? I haven't had a day off in three weeks. I mean if they're gonna call me in at least throw me a bone. Gimme the 419 on the elevator.

Nick: Someone's bitter.

Sara: I'm tired!

Nick: You? Tired? I thought you never sleep. Haha, nice, nice.

Nick: What up, G?

Sara: You're awake. I hate you.

Greg: Couple glasses of Merlot, a rack of lamb on my day off. I slept like a baby yesterday. You look horrible.

Sara: Thanks, Greg.

Nick: Don't look at me. I got 'sunshine' all night. Check for DNA in the sexual assault kit and the fingernail, please.

Sara: Everything has to be in CODIS ASAP.

Greg: Oh, is that all? I want to know who's going to authorize my overtime?

Sara: Suck it up, Greg. You're well-rested.

Greg (to Nick): You want a valium for her?

Sara: I heard that!

Sara: This Chilean sea bass is excellent.

Catherine: So is this.

Sara: Okay, you got your missing widow. Her bloody tooth found in her own

bedroom which is currently occupied by two moes.

Brass: "Moes." I'm rubbing off on you.

Sara: No, you're not, and stay away from my seabass.

Grissom: Who found her?

Brass: Look around you. This is gonna take all night.

Grissom: Come for the hors d'oeuvres... stay for the interrogation.

Catherine: What? Why are you smiling?

Grissom: It's playing our song.

Grissom: Are you looking for work?

Nick: I just...

Grissom: The sign says, "Do Not Enter," Nick. You can't read anymore? You're blind? What?

Nick Grissom, this is important.

Grissom: This is important. Sometimes in interrogations, Nick, you get one chance, one answer. And while I'm out here screwing around with you he's in there thinking up an answer that he didn't have before you walked in.

Nick: We matched the DNA taken from Lacey Duvall to a cold case in Texas ten years ago.

Grissom: And?

Nick: The suspect's name was Chad Matthews.

Grissom: C.M. The cuff link. Okay, I'm starting to forgive you.

Nick: Sara ran Patrick Haynes' social. The real Haynes is deceased. So

Patrick Haynes is Chad Matthews and Chad Matthews is on the run.

Grissom: And he just ran into us.

Grissom: Have you got the DNA results from the fingernail Catherine found?

Greg: Yeah. They're not a match to Patrick Haynes.

Grissom: I never figured a man for the fingernail, Greg.

Greg: But this is where you break out the can of creep repellent. Half of the DNA markers are in common.

Grissom: A possible first degree relative?

Warrick: It's like the Circle Bar on a Friday night - three million people on top of each other.

Sara: No, I can't drink any more coffee. My body clock is so screwed up. I just want a steak and a shot.

Nick: Tut's Tomb, steak and eggs $1.99.

Sara: Food?

Nick: Mmhmm.

Sara: Good idea. You're on.

Greg: It's what I live for. You guys are not gonna believe this. You ready?

Sara: So much for the steak, I'll take the coffee.

Catherine: Well, according to her credit card records Portia Richmond hasn't spent a dime since she's been in the Mediterranean.

Sara: She's dead.

Catherine: Not necessarily. She may have been... swept off her feet.

Nick: Some guys still like to foot the bill.

Sara: Really? How would you know?

Nick: Hey, I only go dutch if girls ask the wrong question.

Catherine: What's that?

Nick: "What do you drive?"

Sara:: It's a honest question.

Nick: No it's not. What it means is "how much do you make so you can take care of me".

Sara: Well, not this girl.

Grissom: The Old Testament? The book of Jonah? And the Lord arranged for a fish to swallow up Jonah. You know what the problem with the piranha, though? They have high cholesterol.

Catherine: Cholesterol is found in humans, not fish. So how does a fish acquire human cholesterol?

Too Tough To Die

This is the sixteenth episode of the first season of CSI Las Vegas.

Synopsis

Security guards in a parking garage are engrossed in watching television. On another level, a woman goes to her car, and a man comes up from behind and puts a gun to her back.

A car drives along and pulls over to investigate a strange figure on the side of the road. It's the woman from the parking garage—she's been beaten and shot but she's still alive.

Sara arrives at the scene with Grissom and Nick. Brass tells them that the victim was a well-dressed black woman, who was shot and beaten. Grissom sends Sara to the hospital to do the rape kit while he and Nick process the scene.

Grissom give Catherine and Warrick a first degree murder case that had belonged to a CSI that quit the day before. Grissom asks to speak to Catherine outside, and tells her that her bank called him about her income because Eddie is trying to take second mortgage out on the house. Catherine is furious.

Sara goes to the hospital to take the rape kit. The Detective tells her that the victim is currently unidentified, and has two bullets in her brain that the doctor can't remove without killing her. Sara looks at her ring finger and says that she is either married or recently divorced, then asks for privacy to do the rape kit, talking to the victim and explaining everything she is doing even though she is comatose.

At the roadside, Nick finds cartridge casings, and Grissom finds a blue jean belt loop that he prepares for use with dogs when they get a better idea of where the suspect is. He tells Nick and Brass that there's a caveat, but doesn't specify what that might be.

Warrick reviews the evidence in their case: A Mr. Hastings lent a Mr. McCall a motorcycle which was returned by McCall with a dent in it. According to McCall, they argued, then Hastings stabbed him with a screwdriver, and McCall defended himself by shooting Hastings twice. Hastings's wife, however, disagrees. She says that McCall shot her husband in the back and that this can be found in the coroner's report. Catherine wants to see the screwdriver, and Warrick tells her that it's missing.

In the lab, Nick give the cartridge casing of the blue jeans belt loop to the lab tech to see if there are any in the database that match, and they appear to have a match.

Sara finishes the rape kit and looks through the victim's clothing; she finds a St. Catherine scapular and presses it in the victim's hand. Grissom arrives at the hospital, and Sara tells him the kit is ready to process; Grissom reminds Sara not to lose track of the fact that the victim herself is evidence, and tells Sara that if you try to chase two rabbits you can end up losing them both.

Catherine and Warrick go to the Hastings house. Mrs. Hastings tells them that she was doing laundry and heard the argument, she went out and saw McCall draw the gun and shoot her husband in the back. Catherine has a few questions to ask Mrs. Hastings about the argument, and this time, she changes her story a bit: she this time says didn't see both shots. She saw the second but she only heard the first shot. Catherine adds that she timed herself running out of the laundry room and it took 3.8 seconds to reach the scene, so there is no way that Mrs. Hastings saw McCall shoot any of the bullets.

Nick and Sara find that the gun used on the victim was used in a gang related shooting. Sara finds a black baseball cap, and Grissom says gang shooters mark their kills by leaving their hats. Sara says she might be able to get DNA from the hat and she could compare them to Jane's—i.e., Jane Doe, the unidentified victim.

Brass and Grissom talk to Det. Sam Vega, from the gang unit. He identifies the cap as belonging to a gang member. They go out canvassing the neighborhood and Grissom tells Nick the caveat: they can't get a warrant for evidence they find using a dog search.

Warrick and Catherine talk to McCall and he says that he was stabbed in the arm. Catherine looks at the stab mark. She tells Warrick that she thinks he's telling the truth; he was stabbed in the right arm, and he's right-handed. If he did it himself, he would have stabbed his left arm, and the would be angled up instead of down. Leaving the prison, Eddie calls, and Catherine asks him about the mortgage. He claims that he told her about it, that he's using the money to get a music studio.

In the morgue, Warrick tells Dr. Robbins that McCall swears that he shot Hastings in the front; Dr. Robbins says he determined that the victim was shot in the back. Warrick comments that when two guys are fighting, there's lots of bobbing and weaving and confusion and moving around, and Dr. Robbins tells him that it's up to the CSIs to put perspective on the crime.

Sara, determined to solve the case, says that the DNA from the cap was a match to the semen from Jane Doe's rape kit. There is no DNA in the system matching either, so she's looking through missing person's reports to try to identify the woman before she dies. Grissom warns her can't get too close to the victims, or else she'll burn out. Sara eventually finds a missing persons report for a Pamela Adler, who was out shopping at the time that she went missing.

Catherine and Warrick look at the t-shirt that Hastings was wearing, and perform experiment using the same gun and ammo to test the distance of the shooting; six inches, 1 foot, 1.5 feet, 2 feet, and check for powder burns that match against shirt. They discover that the first shot matches the shot fired from 2 feet away, and the second matches for a shot fired from 1 foot. Catherine comments that Mrs. Hastings said that her husband was running away when he was shot, but their experiments show that he was moving closer.

Grissom wants to use the dogs, Nick reminds him that they won't be able to get a warrant from any evidence that they find, and they debate as to whether or not using the dogs is better than coming up with nothing at all. In the end, the dogs go out, and lead them to a house where a young teen is playing basketball outside. Nick notes a missing belt loop on his jeans. The boy's mother comes out and asks her son, Tony, what's happening, and acts in a hostile manner towards Grissom and Nick.

Catherine and Warrick set up a mannequin and put straws in to the wound tracks. Warrick says that they were probably fighting with one of them bent in a certain position, and bends the dummy that way. Catherine agrees that that's how it must have happened, and that both witnesses were telling the truth.

Brass questions Tony, and ask if he'll give them his jeans; his mother says that he doesn't have to do anything since they don't have a warrant. Tony says that he has nothing to hide, then adds that the woman isn't even dead, and he's a juvenile anyway. They tell him that if she dies within a year and a day, then he'll be charged with murder no matter how old he was when she was attacked, but he's still not particularly concerned.

Catherine and Warrick come out and find Eddie waiting for Catherine with Lindsey. Warrick takes Lindsey away to his office; Catherine and Eddie argue, and he insults her; she starts to slap him but he grabs her arm. Grissom comes in and orders him to get out and never come back, to which Eddie comments that he always knew that Catherine and Grissom had a thing going.

Catherine and Warrick tell the DA that Hastings was facing McCall but was shot in the back as Hastings lunged at McCall's mid-section. Catherine says that the first shot was self-defense, but the second one wasn't; Hastings was already on the ground. They leave the charge for the DA to determine.

Sara goes to the hospital to visit the victim, sitting on the bed by Jane's side without noticing that a man is sitting in the corner. She tells Pamela that they caught the guy who did this to her all because she had the strength to pull his belt loop off. Mr. Adler, the man sitting in the corner introduces himself to Sara as Pamela's husband, and adds that they'll be moving his wife to a long-term care facility at the end of the week and invites her to come and visit.

Sara cries and talks to Grissom. The victim is going to be vegetative state for the rest of her life, while the kid who did it will be out of juvenile detention in 48 months. Grissom tells her that she has to learn to let it go, and Sara tells him that she wishes she were like him, wishes that she didn't feel anything, and leaves, with Grissom staring after her.

Memorable Quotes

Catherine: You set me up. Again.

Eddie: How, by taking our daughter to dinner?

Catherine: Get over here.

Eddie: Oh, come on now! What?!

Catherine: You are so pathetic. Just so pathetic.

Eddie: Watch it, Cath.

Catherine: Sucking up to our daughter 'cause I caught you robbing me.

Eddie: The only thing I robbed you of is good sex.

Catherine: No sex is worth you. And you are not taking my daughter to a club with one of your music whores.

Eddie: Oh, they're whores? When I met you, you were taking your clothes off in a strip club.

Catherine: It was a job, Ed. And it supported you just like every other job I've had including this one!

Eddie: Yeah? And who paid to close up your nose?

Catherine: You're such a bast...

Catherine: Let go of me.

Eddie: I'll let go of you when I'm damn good and...

Grissom: Let go of her, Ed! Catherine?

Catherine: Just get him out of here.

Grissom: I don't ever wanna see you in this building again. This is our place of business. You understand that?

Eddie: I always knew you two had a thing.

Grissom: Go home, Eddie.

Eddie: Sure. (Walks away)

Warrick: This dummy cost over $500?

Catherine: Oh, yeah. He's worth it.

Warrick: Why?

Catherine: Well, look at him. He's lifelike, he doesn't talk, and he's self-

healing.

Warrick: He's "self-healing"?

Catherine: Yeah. We make a mistake in our calculations we just start over.

Nick: Whoa! (To Grissom) Are we supposed to be able to keep up with those guys?

Grissom: Yeah!

Sara: This sweatband might give us DNA and I could compare it to the samples I collected off of Jane at the hospital.

Grissom: Jane?

Sara: Our....Jane Doe. My "death imminent."

Nick: First-name basis, Sara?

Grissom: Hey.

Sara: Any luck on 23rd street?

Grissom: I, uh, broke in my new shoes. That's about it. What'd the lab say?

Sara: The DNA from the ball cap is a match to the semen we found on our Jane Doe. But ... CODIS hasn't kicked out a name.

Grissom: So you're just...looking at missing person's reports?

Sara: We're not having any luck finding the shooter from his DNA with a belt loop so I thought I would at least try and identify the poor woman before she dies.

Grissom: Sara. Do you have any diversions?

Sara: Do I what?

Grissom: You max out on overtime every month. You go home and listen to your police scanner.

Grissom: You read forensic textbooks...

Sara: Yeah.

Grissom: Look, every day we meet people on the worst day of their lives. It's a lot to deal with. Everyone who's had any time on this job knows that you have to have a diversion in order to cope with what we see. What do you do for fun?

Sara: I chase rabbits. And...I read crime books. And I listen to the scanner.

Grissom: You need something outside of law enforcement. Catherine has her kid, you know? I sometimes...ride roller coasters.

Grissom: What do you do?

Sara: Nothing.

Grissom: Okay. What do you like?

Sara: I don't like anything.

Grissom: You've got to find something to like. You can't get too close to the victims.

Sara: She's special...to me. I can't help it.

Grissom: If you don't find something they'll all become special and you'll burn out.

Nick: Now you want to use the dogs to track down the Jane Doe shooter?

Grissom: K-9 units going to meet us there.

Nick: Yeah, but I spoke to Brass. He said we can't get a warrant on anything we need from the suspect's house-- gun, jeans, nothing.

Grissom: That's if we find him inside his house. In which case, we'll figure out another way to get a warrant.

Nick: You're rushing this for Sara.

Grissom: My priority is the case, Nick. Release the hounds.

Nick: Still, you'd think the bad guys would figure we'd eventually start a database on cartridge casings, huh?

Grissom: Locard's principal. He took a piece of her away with him and he left a piece of himself here. We get to find it.

(Catherine and Warrick are carrying some boxes for Grissom)
Grissom: Thank you, my sherpas.

Nick: Hey, Sara, did anyone ever tell you, you have a pretty good singing voice?
Sara: If you like chalk on a board!

Shandra Thorpe: You police.. coming here with your attack dogs.
Grissom: Actually, they're scent dogs, and I'm not a police officer. I'm a Forensic Scientist with the Las Vegas Police Department.
Shandra Thorpe: What do I got to say to a scientist?
Grissom: You could say "hello."

Warrick: Hey...when's the last time you took target practice?
Catherine: Figures. I just had a manicure.

Warrick: Oh, you are wrong!

Nick: Our ball cap belongs to somebody in this neighborhood. These houses are full of people who know the guy who wears it.

Brass: Okay, Nick, ready to burn some shoe leather? Some old-fashioned police work? What do you say, huh?

Nick: Why can't we just use those scent pads?

Grissom: The dogs? Constitutional issue. We can't get a warrant for the evidence we find off the dogs' search.

Nick: Great, great. Why'd you even suggest it?

Grissom: You're a grown man, Nick. Stop whining.

Grissom: If you try and chase two rabbits you end up losing them both.

Sara: The husband doesn't get it. He's so happy she's going to live. He doesn't realize she's going to be in a vegetative state for the rest of her life. And that kid Thorpe...is going to be out of juvie in 48 months. It's not fair.

Grissom: It's the system.

Sara: What kind of system rewards the suspect when the victim is too tough to die?

Grissom: Sara...you got to learn to let this go or you're going to spend all your time in hospitals trying to help the people you couldn't save.

Sara: I wish I was like you, Grissom. I wish I didn't feel anything.

Face Lift

This is the seventeenth episode of the first season of CSI Las Vegas.

Synopsis

A couple begins their day by opening their pottery store. Inside, things are broken; the man sees a body on the floor and tells the woman to call 9-1-1.

Grissom, Catherine and Nick arrive at the store. They soon learn that the deceased is Joseph Felton, aged 44, and that he was not an employee or former employee. Nick notices a burn mark on the safe from which the cash was taken, and has contusions on the back of his skull. This means the robber is also a homicide victim.

Dr. Robbins tells them that death was instantaneous and that he was hit on the head. He also had a yellow substance and some glitter on his head that have been sent to the lab for analysis. Catherine combs fern spores from the hair of the victim, and Nick comments that the back entrance of the store was overgrown with them.

Grissom tells Catherine that he's identified one finger print from the scene that came up in the database: Melissa Marlowe, who was kidnapped over 20 years ago. The print, however, was few weeks old. The case has now become two cases. Grissom takes the kidnapping, and Catherine and Nick take the homicide.

At a house that is the scene of another potential homicide, Sara and Warrick examine the remains of a woman who was incinerated while sitting in a chair. She was reduced to ashes leaving only her foot behind, and the fire created a chimney for itself by burning a hole in the ceiling.

At the station, Mr. Winston, the husband of the incinerated woman, tells O'Riley that he has no idea what happened to his wife-- when he went to bed she was asleep in the chair, and when he got up, she was ashes. He didn't know that she hadn't come to bed because they sleep separately—Mrs. Winston snored.

Brass shows Nick photos of a crime scene from 1999 where a safe was broken into using a plasma lance. There were two perps in this particular robbery: Joseph Felton and Darin Hanson. Joseph flipped and testified against Darin Hanson, who was finally just recently released from prison. Brass and Nick think that he and Felton got together to commit this crime, and once the safe was open, Hanson killed Joseph Felton as revenge for testifying against him. They bring Hanson in for questioning. He says he was in Barstow all week, and has receipts to prove it. The receipts look authentic, and so they let him go.

Grissom talks to Mr. and Mrs. Marlowe and tells them that their daughter is possibly still alive. Teri Miller says she will use an old picture to age Melissa's face so they can see what she'd look like today.

In the morgue, Catherine takes Tammy Felton to view the body of her father, Joseph. As she looks at the body, she begins to cry, and tells Catherine that she has no other family. As Tammy turns away, Catherine notices some fern spores on her jacket and pulls a few of them off of her. She asks if Tammy was at the pottery store with her father, saying that the spores place both of them at the scene of the crime. Tammy admits that she was there, but says that she went to stop him and he told her to leave, so she did.

Warrick asks Dr. Robbins for any information on Mrs. Winston's foot and Dr. Robbins says that the ankle bone is hollowed out, which means that it was burned off the body, not severed.

Teri Miller uses the computer to age the childhood picture of Melissa Marlowe. Catherine looks at the picture once it's been completed, and says that it's Tammy Felton, and wonders if she murdered the man who kidnapped her to seek revenge. Grissom and Catherine visit Dr. Kane, a psychiatrist, who tells them that Tammy/Melissa might remember something of her life before she was kidnapped, and children like that often show sociopathic behavior; Catherine comments that Tammy/Melissa needs help as she's a victim of kidnapping as well as a suspect in a murder case. Grissom tells Catherine to talk to Tammy again, and Dr. Kane warns her that sociopaths can be very dangerous.

Sara tells Warrick that there's no evidence of foul play in Mrs. Winston's death, and that there is no insurance money to provide a motivation for the murder. Testing has not even shown that there was an accelerant involved. The only way she could have burned, according to the clues they've gathered, was through spontaneous combustion.

Greg and Nick check the swab taken from Joseph Felton's head for mineral content and turns out to be a trace amount of uranium. The amount is so small that it can't harm Greg or Nick, but whatever the murder weapon is, it has uranium on or in it. Because oxidized uranium used to be used as a color enhancer in paints and dyes, it's likely that it came from something in the pottery store. Nick returns to the store with a Geiger counter to check the items, and finds that a gnome sets off the counter—a gnome with a chip out of the side of it, and hair and blood at the base.

In an interview room, Catherine interviews Tammy and asks about her mother. Tammy is under the impression that her mother's name was Mara, and she died a few years back. Grissom tells the Marlowes that they can see Melissa but not talk to her, and takes them to the interview room where they watch from the other side of a one way mirror, and listen to her talk about her childhood. As Tammy leaves, Mrs. Marlowe runs after her, calling her Melissa, and hugs her. Tammy doesn't recognize her mother, and tells her that she's not her daughter and leaves. Catherine tells the Marlowes that Melissa now identifies as Tammy Felton; Mr. Marlowe tells them that Mara Felton was their babysitter.

Sara meets Warrick behind the labs with a cotton nightgown like Mrs. Winston was wearing, and a pig to Warrick has a pig. Warrick says that they're going to use the pig to figure out what happened, adding that Mrs. Winston was a could have set herself on fire. Sara tells him that it this were the case, Mrs. Winston would have woken up, but Warrick says that there was Seconal in her system.

Catherine, Nick, and Grissom arrive at Tammy's house with a warrant. Nick finds a pair of gloves that have yellow, uranium based paint on them. Tammy claims that she never wore the gloves; they were her mother's, so Grissom cuts them open and dusts the inside for finger prints while Catherine prints Tammy. There is a visual match between the two sets of prints. Grissom speculates that Joseph lanced the safe, and once it was open, Tammy bashed him on the head with the gnome. Tammy says that she didn't kill her father, and that they weren't alone in the store during the robbery. Grissom tells her that there's no evidence of a third person being present and Tammy insists that there was – a woman named Melissa Marlowe, and she was the one who killed him.

They consult with Dr. Kane on the issues surrounding multiple personalities. He tells them that the dominant personality (Tammy) would know both, but the other (Melissa) might not. Mr. and Mrs. Marlowe show up with a lawyer for Melissa.

In the interview room, Mrs. Marlowe calls her Melissa, but she says that she's Tammy, and continues to insist that

Joseph was her father and Mara her mother. Tammy looks at the necklace that Mrs. Marlowe is wearing; Mrs. Marlowe tells her that she used to play with it when she was a baby.

Outside, Sara and Warrick play chess while the pig smolders. As it turns out, body fat burns away like candle wax, and that the cotton nightgown acted as a wick.

Catherine goes to see Melissa/Tammy in the cells, and she now identifies as Melissa. She says that she was insane when she killed Joseph Felton, and her only memories are of being a child, and the last 21 years are blank. Catherine tells her that if that's the case, then she should have no memories of her; Catherine would be a stranger. She then tells her that there is no Melissa. Tammy tells her to get out, and as Catherine leaves, Tammy begs her in a sad little-girl voice to come back. Catherine turns and looks at her, and Tammy says, "Just practicing for court... not bad, huh?"

Catherine goes in to Grissom's office and he tells her Tammy skipped bail and left town, adding that the Marlowes lost their house and life savings, as they'd posted bail for her. Catherine has officers check on credit card purchases that the Marlowes made in the last 24 hours.

She and Brass go to the Marlowe's home and Catherine tells them that they know from checking credit card records that they bought 22 bus tickets to 22 different destinations. Brass tells them that if they tell where they were supposed to meet their daughter, and they apprehend Melissa, then they won't press charges, but otherwise, it's a felony. Mrs. Marlowe refuses to tell them anything.

On the roadside, a bus pulls over and a car pulls up to pick up the woman who got off the bus. The driver is Darin Hanson. Tammy tells him that he owes her one since she killed Joseph, but he points out that he's the one who told her that Joseph kidnapped her, so they're even. He asks her where she is going, and she tells him that it doesn't matter.

Memorable Quotes

Nick: Which is radioactive. Do we need to evacuate the building or anything?
Greg: The amount is trace. We should be fine.
Nick: You sure?
Greg No.

Nick: Do you have the results on the swab yet?
Greg: Uh ...

Nick: Uh... from the dead guy at the pottery store? The coroner sent over a sample. You were supposed to analyze the mineral content.

Greg: Oh, yeah, I'm sorry. Grissom has just been running me around like a lapdog. I haven't had a chance.

Nick: Grissom's on a missing persons.. he hasn't sent you anything.

Greg: Did I say Grissom? No, I meant Catherine.

Nick: Oh, yeah. Catherine's working with me.

Greg: Oh. Well, what do you say we check out that swab then, huh?

Nick: Great.

Greg: Don't you ever goof off, huh? Do you ever get a little lost in life?

Nick: No.

Catherine: Hey, Doc, you have a comb?

Nick: Your hair looks great, Cath.

Catherine: Gee, thanks, Nick.

Nick: I should get a finders fee. Here, one for each of you.

Grissom: You and I have an appointment with our shrink.

Warrick: Oh, you're only siding with Sara because you have a crush on her.

Dr. Robbins: No, that's why I wore a clean coat.

Grissom: I think our robbery suspect just became our homicide victim.

Catherine: Well that's one way to avoid the rap.

Grissom: I have a question.

Teri: Ok?

Grissom: Since I screwed up our last date, would we ever have dinner again?

Teri: Oh we'll have dinner... just not together.

Sara: Interesting voicemail you left me.

Warrick: What's that?

Sara: Meet me behind CSI and bring a night gown? I'll wear it for you but uh, I prefer pajamas.

Grissom: I hear that Greg found uranium on the swab from Felton's skull.

Nick: Yeah, he says I'm okay, but you know Greg. Tell me, am I radiating a green glow?

35K OBO

This is the 18th episode of the first season of CSI Las Vegas.

Synopsis

At night, a man and woman come out of a restaurant where they have just celebrated their 8th anniversary. They walk towards their car and as they approach their vehicle, the woman is grabbed from behind and her throat is slit.

At the scene, the woman is near the curb, the man is in the middle of the road, and the car that was between them is missing. Nick examines the man and finds a stray red hair on him that belonged to someone else. As the team begins to examine the scene, a raindrop falls and then a torrential desert storm begins. They have only a few minutes to collect evidence before the rain washes everything away. The team photographs the scene, and tries to bag as much as possible.

After the rain stops, they return to the scene. Grissom asks Brass if there are any eyewitnesses. There is: one, Justin Greene who got blood on his shirt when he went to help the male victim. He says that he was crossing the street and was almost hit by an SUV, and after it had passed, he saw the male victim lying in the street. He gets upset as he recounts the story, telling them that he screwed up--he forgot to tilt his head or clear his airways. Sara asks Justin to turn over his clothes to them, as they have the victim's blood on them.

At a collapsed apartment building, EMT workers attend to injured people. Catherine and O'Riley arrive, and he tells her that part of the basement caved in, killing three old women in their apartment.

In the lab, Nick finds Greg examining the DNA of a woman that he went on a date with last night. He gives Greg the hair from the male victim's body and Greg tells him it's a cat hair.

In the morgue, Dr. Robbins tells Grissom the victims have been ID'd as Kevin Shepherd and his wife Amy. Kevin has 6 stab wounds in his body and Amy's throat was slit. Kevin was attacked with two different weapons; one that was long, sharp and double-edge, which had a smooth entry, and the other which was blunt and left bruising around the points of entry.

Inside the building, Catherine asks for the District Engineer, Paul Newsome. She explains that there are three people dead because the building collapsed. He tells her that he was the last to examine the building and certify it. She wants to examine the origin of the collapse, which is in the laundry room, in the basement.

Sara tells Grissom that Kevin was a chiropractor and Amy a dentist, and they were married for eight years. The eye-witness, Justin Greene, was observed trying to perform CPR on Kevin, so he is not listed as a suspect in the case. Meanwhile, Warrick mixes plaster to make castings of the wounds. Soon, Grissom is called because the highway patrol have found the Shepherd's SUV.

The SUV is on the roadside. The rain would have washed away any evidence on the outside of the vehicle, but there may be evidence on the inside. He opens the driver side door and a woman's body spills out into his arms. The contents of her wallet identify her as Jessica Hall, and her cell phone, which is turned off, has no outbound 911 calls. Grissom finds a red hair on her clothing--the same red cat hair that was found on Kevin Shepherd, but not Amy Shepherd.

At the apartment building, Catherine and Paul Newsome argue briefly when Catherine informs them that a negligent leak-checker can be blamed for a sinking ship. Newsome comments that she must not be married, then guesses that she's divorced. On her way into the building, O'Riley makes sure that she understands the political implications of what she may find: that the Mayor ran on a platform of urban renewal, so if anything bad is found, it will reflect badly on the Mayor, and that could lead to trouble for them.

In the morgue, Dr. Robbins tells Grissom that Jessica Hall's cause of death was a laceration to the liver. As they examine the body, they find a metal fragment lodged in her ribs—it's the tip of the knife that was used to stab her.

Catherine crawls through the basement, and finds a huge bug, which she collects to take to Grissom since he's got a penchant for insects. In the laundry room, she finds the support columns. One of them has been hit, possibly by a sledgehammer.

Once the knife tip has been extracted from the body, Sara and Brass learn from a pawn shop owner that it came from a carbon steel dagger. He then says that a dagger is usually about five inches long, and shows them a knife to similar to what they should be looking for.

In the lab, they match the dagger tip to the clean wounds on Kevin's body, but that still leaves the blunt wounds unidentified. Warrick, after close examination of the knife and the castings, says that the killer started with Kevin, then stabbed Jessica, then went back to Kevin to finish the job; Grissom points out that they now have one weapon and one killer.

Grissom identifies the beetle that Catherine collected from the collapsed building, saying that it eats soft wood; she says that the columns were made of Douglas Fir and suffering from dry rot, and then shows Grissom the sledgehammer marks on the column.

Warrick and Sara examine the SUV, and after taking prints, Sara confirms that Jessica Hall was the last person to drive the vehicle. Nick remarks that all of Kevin's wounds were to the torso, but there is blood spatter on the left instep of Kevin's shoe, which is odd. Nick comments that Amy was too far away, and Jessica was the only other one who was possibly there. Warrick lies on the floor, and Sara kneels over him. This position matches with the blood pattern that is on the shoe but it is unclear as to whether or not she is helping or hindering in that position. Nick suggests that Jessica was helping the killer by holding Kevin down, and that the stab wounds that Jessica sustained may have been accidental. Grissom tells them to get a warrant for Jessica's home.

In the lab, Catherine examines the column and Paul Newsome arrives. He tells her that five years ago, a tenant in the building, Blake Neverson from apartment 204, damaged the column and was charged for it; it's all a matter of public record. At the time, there wasn't enough damage to be of concern, so the building passed inspection. Catherine advises him to explain that to the three dead women.

Brass, Grissom and Nick arrive at Jessica' s home. The lab has confirmed that it was Jessica's blood on Kevin's shoe, and there was a call on Kevin's cell phone to Jessica. Grissom bags a blank pad of paper that is sitting by the computer, and they see a cat whose hair matches that found on Kevin and Jessica. Brass says that he'll have the phone records run to see how often Kevin and Jessica talked to each other to see if they may have had a relationship. Grissom and Nick log on to her banking site with the help of a post-it note by the computer that gives her log in information. They find one deposit for $35,000 from Kevin Shepherd. Jessica moved the money out of the account the same day, but the account that it was moved to hasn't been posted yet. It appears for some reason that Kevin Shepherd paid to have himself and his wife killed.

Nick has some tests run on the blank pad that Grissom found by the computer in Jessica's apartment. From the impressions left on the pad's surface, they find a note that reads "Andres, 9 p.m." which is where Kevin and Amy had dinner. Grissom comments that it looks like Kevin was planning to have his wife murdered, but he wasn't supposed to die, nor was Jessica. A handwriting comparison shows that Kevin Shepherd wrote the note. Brass arrives and tells them that Kevin and Jessica spoke on the phone every day, according to the phone records, but after the last time they were ever to speak on the phone together, Jessica called someone else.

Sara and Warrick find the clothes that Justin Greene turned over to them. Looking at his shirt, they see the mark of someone's hand on his shirt. Grissom has a transparency of Kevin Shepherd's hand and matches it to the print on the shirt. Sara comments that Justin said that he performed CPR, but if Kevin grabbed his shirt, then he didn't need CPR.

Catherine goes to the apartment building and as she stands there, some planes fly by overhead. She goes back to the lab and sets up an experiment: she puts a section of the floor with the support column in a tank with rubber balls and stereo speakers and cranks up the volume on the speakers. The nails in the support column begin to rotate from to the vibrations of the music. The F-16s that fly ahead so frequently might be responsible as they'd do the same thing that the music did. 50 years of fly-bys could have loosened the nails , and that, along with the beetles, dry rot, and sabotage caused the collapse. She tells Paul he's off the hook.

Grissom has the bank documents for all of the people involved in the stabbing: Kevin Shepherd transferred $35,000 to Jessica's account, which Jessica then transferred to Justin Greene's account. Jessica and Justin once had a joint account, and also had the same last name. The next day Amy Shepherd transferred $70,000 to Justin Greene's account. Justin had called Amy before that transfer took place. They speculate that Kevin had hired Jessica, and Jessica had hired Justin. Justin then called Amy and told her what was happening, and she doubled the amount to pay him to kill Kevin instead of her. Justin then decided to keep all the money and kill them both. Jessica may have tried to stop him from stabbing Kevin, but Justin stabbed her, breaking off the knife tip, and then went back to stabbing Kevin. Jessica managed to get to the SUV and drive off, but had been fatally stabbed, so didn't get very far. Once Kevin was dead, Justin discarded the knife down a sewer drain, and then pretended to do CPR on him.

In the interview room, Grissom and Brass talk to Justin. Brass comments that the Shepherds looked like the perfect couple; Grissom comments that looks can kill.

Memorable Quotes

Sara: Justin, we need to take your clothes.
Justin: Why?
Sara: ...'Cause there is blood all over them.

Gil: I used to say 'never' on Sunday, then Harbor happened... I never say never.

Grissom: Well, I haven't felt that in a while.
Brass: What's that?
Grissom: The element of surprise.

Brass: Hey, Warrick. Is Grissom around?
Warrick: You see him?
Brass: You know between you and me, as long as I've been on the job I still don't like touching dead bodies.
Warrick: Well, that's why you got the badge and I got the syringe.

Sara: We're losing everything!

Grissom: Yeah... our killer got lucky tonight.

Paul Newsome: You're not married, are you?

(Catherine looks up and stares at him)

Paul Newsome: Divorced.

Catherine: Is that from the rain?

Paul Newsome: Depends on who's asking.

Catherine: Are you hiding something or am I not worth your time?

Paul Newsome: Excuse me?

Catherine: Well, you are the district engineer of the city, right? You're responsible for the structural safety of this building.

Paul Newsome: I'm sorry, I didn't catch your name.

Catherine: Catherine Willows. Las Vegas Crime Lab.

Paul Newsome: Crime lab?

Catherine: Yeah. The building fell down. Three people were crushed to death.

Catherine: And you're not calling this a crime scene?

O'Riley: Catherine, it's a building!

Catherine: O'Riley ... it's a suspect!

Sara: What's missing here?

Warrick: No car.

Nick: No mercy.

Grissom: Okay. How did her blood get on his shoe?

Nick: Gravity. Warrick, please, on the floor on your back.

Warrick: Man, why are you always trying to put me down?

Brass: I still can't believe you messed up the crime scene.

Grissom: The body fell out when I opened the door. It happens. We move on.

Brass: Uh-huh. It's gonna bother you all day.

Paul Newsome: Look, lady, I don't know what it is...

Catherine: Catherine.

Paul Newsome: Sorry.

Catherine: Don't say "Sorry". Just know who you're talking to.

Grissom: Our little Jessica was a prolific note-taker. "Try to be a good person today."

Brass: Yeah, right. Try not to kill too many people.

Nick: Pulled a couple of hairs off of our male stabbing vic.

Greg: Okay. Baby. Uh-huh.

Nick: What?

Greg: Nine lives.

Nick: Cat hair?

Greg: Meow.

Nick: Hey, Greg.

Greg: Shh. I might be looking at the mother of my children here.

Nick: Somebody's been putting in way too much overtime.

Greg: No, this is serious. I had a date last night. And this girl has the most impossible green eyes. Just, BAM. Shoulder-length blonde hair, intelligent. And she smells so good.

Nick: Cute toes?

Greg: Oh, ideal. And none longer than the big toe. Both feet. But you know I need to know is what is on the inside.

Nick: What's in her heart?

Greg: No, her DNA. This girl has got some fine epithelials.

Nick: Dude, you're sick. Man, you have officially lost it.

Greg: There's a guy in Louisville, he charges 300 clams to test your spouse's underwear for foreign DNA. Now that guy is sick. I'm just a romantic.

Nick: Whatever happened to getting to know someone over coffee? Letting the relationship evolve. Romantic is sending flowers, not bogarting her skin cells.

Greg: Oh that's boring.

Grissom: Ya know what they say about looks.

Brass: They can be deceiving?

Grissom: They can kill.

Grissom: Don't forget to feed him.
Catherine: I know, wood.

"Gentle, Gentle"

This is the 19th episode of the first season of CSI Las Vegas.

Synopsis

The episode opens at night, starting with an exterior shot of a typically Vegas nouveau riche colonial McMansion.

In the master bedroom, a woman leaps out of bed and races down the hall to a baby's nursery. The window is open and the curtain flaps in the breeze. The crib is empty and there is a neatly typed ransom note that reads "I have your son. I don't want to harm him. Don't make me. I'll call in six hours with instructions. I advise you not to call the police."

Gil, Brass, and Catherine arrive at the house and thread their way through the black and whites that have arrived. They are led to the empty crib and ask the father for the ransom note. He at first seems puzzled as to why law enforcement would actually want to see the note that was left by the criminal that took his son, but eventually finds it and produces it.

CSI gets the phones set up so that they can monitor the parents' phone call with the kidnapper and get a trace on it. Before they start the call, however, Grissom seems unsettled by a half-empty coke bottle and takes it from the husband, Mr. Anderson, and then notes that the thermostat reads 72 degrees.

"Mrs. Anderson" -- replays her version of events: she got up at 4:30 in the morning to feed baby Zack, and when she went into his room, he was gone. Her husband then came in, saw what happened, and called the police. Gil asks for a piece of Zack's clothing so they can use scent dogs through the neighborhood. Grissom then asks for DNA samples from everyone in the house they can more easily identify the DNA evidence left by an outsider. tells the room's remaining occupants he'd like blood samples from all the family members.

The dogs are being led into the house, and Gil instructs Sara to take the ransom note to Questioned Documents, and then asks Nick to take the unopened soda to the lab, in a controlled space, 72 degrees Fahrenheit and open it, and keep the opened soda in the same room temp space. Warrick canvasses the exterior ,and photographs the print left on the base of the ladder that was up against the baby's window, and is noticeably interested in the spider web that would have obstructed the passage of a would-be kidnapper. Grissom, meanwhile, finds a long black hair in the crib and takes it, and then sprays for blood and finds a lot of it on the walls.

Back at CSI Central, the lab tech has identified a quirk in the printer used to make the ransom note, but hasn't yet fingerprinted it.

As Warrick and Grissom continue surveying the house, the dogs begin barking, and they sprint over to see what they found: the body of the baby wrapped in a white blanket and lying on a plastic drop cloth at the foot of a statue. Catherine and Mrs. Anderson are right behind them and Mrs. Anderson begins to wail.

The coroner tells Grissom that the baby appeared to be suffocated, and his sternum was cracked.

Back at Anderson home, Grissom talks to the distraught parents about his progress in solving the case. He doesn't believe that a stranger has done this to their child. Mr. Anderson, who feels that he is being accused, gets upset. Grissom points out that the family never received a call from the kidnapper, which is odd, considering that the kidnapper seemed motivated to turn a profit, and family clearly has money to burn. Warrick then informs them that the blood they found in the baby's room belongs to the oldest Anderson boy, Tyler.

Tyler explains that he broke a window playing ball, cut himself trying to clean it up, and leaked blood all over the floor. The CSI team is not necessarily buying it, and search the house, finding a pair of grass-stained pantyhose and an empty blanket wrapper.

Nick, meanwhile, has been at the lap, keeping a log of the pressure released from the control bottle every quarter-hour, and realized that there was ethanol/alcohol on the lip of the opened bottle. noted the presence of ethanol (a.k.a. booze) on the lip of the already-opened bottle. Grissom, pleased, gives him the blanket wrapper and the nylons to analyze.

They also get the results of the prints back from the lab. The letter has three sets of prints on it: Mrs. Anderson, Mr. Anderson, and Mr. Anderson's secretary, Needra Fenway. Her printer, matches the quirks of the printer that rattled off the ransom note.

Needra is immediately brought in for interrogation. Grissom asks her why her printer was used for the ransom note, and asks why her hair was found in Zach's crib.

Eventually, she admits that she and Mr. Anderson were having an affair but that it ended when his wife was pregnant. Catherine accuses her of killing the baby, but she denies it.

Grissom then returns to the Anderson home to talk to the husband. He insists that Needra was not the culprit of the baby's kidnapping, but that her hair got in the crib because she wanted to see the baby to get concrete evidence that the affairs was over. Grissom snaps at him, and tells him he has evidence that the soda bottle was not opened immediately after the police were called, as Mr. Anderson said, it was opened at 11 pm the night before and cut with rum. He continues to ask: "Was Needra Fenway in your house that night? Did you catch her suffocating your son?" Mr Anderson, without much finesse, replies: "That's not how it happened!" They are interrupted when his toddler, Robbie drops a glass, and begins crying when his father yells at him.

Grissom isn't able to continue after that, because Needra has sold photos of herself with Mr. Anderson to a tabloid to cover her legal expenses, and a reporter asks Mr. Anderson to comment.

Later, we learn that Gwen Anderson hospitalized her oldest son Tyler when he was a toddler for shaking him. CNN just dug up a thirteen-year-old charge against Gwen Anderson. It's called shaken-baby syndrome. The oldest boy, Tyler, when he was a baby, she shook him so hard he had to go to the hospital. She shook the kid unconscious." Catherine asks about the authenticity of the report, and Brass shows her a report faxed from Oregon.

Gwen Anderson is again called in for questioning, and is tailed by reporters and a mob screaming "baby killer" at her. When inside, she tells Catherine and Grissom what happened to Tyler: she was a young and inexperienced mother. Grissom interrupts to inform her that the golf course she lives on paints its grass with vegetable dye, and brandishes her stained nylons. Her lawyer instructs her not to answer questions and leads her off. Gil and Catherine watch her head out to her husband and kids. Soon thereafter, Sara tells Grissom that the lab tech isolated the fiber found in Zachary's throat. It's a flame-retardant fabric called Metamarid. It's not a common fiber for flame-retardant infant clothes, but something stronger, commonly used on things meant to be used near fire and flames.

Gil returns to the Anderson home, arriving there before they do, and finds a potholder that is the same color as the fiber in Zach's throat.

Warrick, meanwhile, is breaking down the Anderson's 911 call with a machine that measures stress levels in people's voices. s he breaks down the Andersons' 911 call. His analysis has concluded that the mother's stress is genuine. This still, however, doesn't clear Tyler.

The Andersons meet with the CSIs at seven the next morning and after being pressed by CSI Gwen gives a confession: Zach wouldn't stop crying, she snapped, and she suffocated the baby with a pot holder. Gil goes on to state that Zachary died while in Tyler's babysitting care earlier that night, but Gwen interrupts and details how she suffocated her baby, while Tyler drops his head in his hands and shakes it no repeatedly.

Warrick, however, disagrees with her confession. He saw that Tyler had called 911 with his cell phone. There is a call featuring Tyler "Robbie! What did you do? What did you do?" over and over again.

In the next scene, Tyler tells what really happened: he was watching the boys, but he got on the phone with his girlfriend and when he turned back, Robbie was suspiciously quiet and Zach was already dead. Robbie had somehow suffocated him by dropping a pot holder on his face. When the parents arrived home, Tyler was doing CPR on his brother but it was no use. "We wanted to protect Robbie. We didn't want him to grow up with the stigma of 'the boy who killed his brother,'" Mr. Anderson says.

Catherine says "Now I know why you didn't want to hold Robbie when your husband handed him to you outside the police department. I'm very sorry."

Memorable Quotes

Warrick: I'm all over it like a cheap suit.

Grissom: Have you let anyone else touch this note? Police, a relative, anyone?
Dad: No, just us. Why?
Grissom: Well, because the person who touched it before you has your son, and he's just left us the first piece of the puzzle.

Gwen Anderson: He was choking.
Brass: All on his own?

Brad Lewis: Change your tone or I'll end this right now.

Brass: Well, it's a legitimate question. But I have to work on my tone. You're right. I'll try again. All on his own?

Catherine: A guy cheats, but the wife commits murder. How come moms always end up the bad guy with you Freud types?

Brass: Geez. Haven't these people ever heard of divorce?

Sara: You told me a few weeks ago that nothing is personal. No victim should be special. Everyone follows your lead.

Grissom: Everyone didn't find that baby. I did. And that little boy is dead because someone lost their temper or screwed up, or god knows what. So, excuse me, but this victim is special.

Nick: No, thanks, I'm an iced tea man.

Catherine: Ice.

Grissom: I don't need this.

Catherine: Just do it.

Catherine: You're an average family, burdened with a tragedy that put you under a microscope. That close, nobody can look good

Sounds of Silence

This is the twentieth episode of the first season of CSI Las Vegas.

Synopsis

The show opens with two scantily clad and drunk women driving through the side streets of Las Vegas, apparently lost. The car thumps and experiences some turbulence and they debate if it was a pothole, or if the driver hit someone.

Grissom, Sara, and Warrick arrive. Grissom draws back the body's sweatshirt, then notices the tire treads arrayed perpendicularly on the body's torso. The fact that the tread marks are under the sweatshirt, and wider than the car's tires, indicates that the women ran over a dead body.

Nick and Catherine meet them at the scene to tell them that they are rolling to a shooting at the Vegas Grounds Coffee Shop with multiple fatalities, and continue on their way.

At the morgue, the technician has identified the deceased as Brian Clemonds, 22 years old, born in Las Vegas, and

Deaf-he was printed as part of a state aid program in '81, and the coroner examined the inner ear to confirm.

Grissom notes that there's a college for the Deaf in Las Vegas about a mile from where Brian was found. They are tempted to think that Brian went out for a walk, was hit by the first car, and then by the car full of party girls, but the coroner points out that Brian's bloodied knuckles don't have any relation to the injuries one sustains when one is hit by a car, and that the blood is not his anyway

Meanwhile, at the coffee shop, it looks like a massacre. Brass enters as Catherine stops at a male body, one of Frankie Flynn, former owner of the Orpheus. Since the cash register is still intact -- as are the picturesque sacks of coffee beans -- Brass is positing that whoever shot up the place didn't do it for money. Catherine conjectures that if it was a hit on Flynn, the shooter followed Flynn through the front door, shot the muscle first, then Flynn, then a patron, then the barristas.

At around this time, Grissom goes to the parents of Brian Clemonds to tell them about heir son, that not only is he dead, but they think he might have been murdered.

And at the morgue, the coroner begins to process the bodies, starting with Frankie Flynn. He sustained gunshot wounds to the head and stomach and actually was suffering from colon cancer at the time of his death. Twenty-year-old Erin McCarty died the same way, but was in the early stages of pregnancy.

The next day, Sara and Warrick visit the college for the Deaf in Las Vegas to talk to the president, Dr. Gilbert. Sara and Warrick, speaking to her through the ASL interpreter when asking questions of Dr. Gilbert, are upbraided for doing so when she snaps: "I'm severely deaf and I can communicate fine. I'd appreciate it if you look at me when you speak to me. I wear a hearing aid, and I can read lips. You could have asked if I needed an interpreter." Sara apologizes, and then asks to see the records of the deceased, but Dr. Gilbert is upset and demands that they send someone else who is more sensitive and understanding of the school and her students, and kicks them out,.

At CSI, Grissom asks Sara for a report and she angrily explains that she was kicked out for not having a warrant. She goes on to explain that she was hostile to them, adding "Like it's our fault we can hear," Sara says, and Grissom says he'll accompany them back to the campus. He barges in to Dr. Gilbert's office and introduces himself, informing her of what she already knew: "You kicked my people out of your office." She begins to kick him out too until Grissom, who knows everything about bugs and forensics, also seems to have picked up a little sign language. He says to her: "Your student is dead. Don't you want to know who's responsible? I do."

They spar back and forth and she accuses his team of seeing her just as a deaf person and nothing else. Finally, she is placated when the team agrees to include her in their investigation. Finally they get a peek at his files. As it turns out, the school failed to move Brian away from his violent roommate Paul Arrington, despite Brian filing six complaints. Paul, as it turns out, lost his hearing less than a year ago, doesn't read lips, doesn't sign, and is having a rough time adjusting, leading him to have uncontrollable outbursts.

Later, Catherine stops by his office. She had asked him to do paperwork so that she could go to the American Association Meeting in Chicago, but he forgot and missed the deadline. She gets upset and he looks truly apologetic. After letting him feel bad for a few seconds, she says the deadline was actually tomorrow because she knew he'd forget.

Sara and Warrick look at tire treads from Brian's torso that have been scanned so they can be matched against a database. Warrick is looking at Brian's clothes and he notices a louse. After digging through his scalp, Warrick concludes that Brian's attackers had lice. Soon after, a discovery is mad: Brian Kendall used to be a waiter at Jimmy Flynn's casino and he has a gun.

The lab tech has also come up with something: a glowing blue pigment called pyoverdin-- a bacteria found in bodies of water, soil and certain plants and animal tissue. Sara also matched partial serial number of a taillight found at the scene to the tread, and they've got a vehicle: a Ford Explorer -- a P235-75 –and there is only one of those registered in Las Vegas. It is registered to 18-year-old Adam Walkey, and vehicle is infested with lice.

Adam is brought in for questioning, and they take a blood sample and examine him for lice. In a twist: he doesn't have it. He does have P. aeruginosa, though.

As Catherine and Nicky continue their investigation, they learn that the guys weren't killed first; the girls were. Also, they learn that the pregnant girl lived with her mother and didn't tell her that she was pregnant. They head down to the morgue to get a DNA sample from the fetus.

Undeterred by the fact that Adam does not have lice, Sara and Grissom examine the SUV. Sara notices a piece of Brian's sweater caught on the muffler, and Warrick concludes that the car may have been driving backwards when it hit Brian. Grissom drags Adam back into questioning. He insists that it wasn't murder—it was a hit-and-run, aka vehicular manslaughter. They counter his claim by noting that since he didn't have lice, but it's in the SUV, someone in the car with him had it. They ask who was in the car, and if that person can corroborate that it was an accident.

As for the coffee house: they found out that a Brian Kendall's ammo was used. They go to question the suspect, and get his DNA.

Mark Rucker, the other guy in the SUV who has lice, is now being questioned. He says they were so busy driving fast and arguing over the radio that they didn't realize they'd hit someone. Gil doesn't buy it, asking how Mark's lice got on the body. Gil wheedles out the truth: the boys asked him to buy liquor for them because they were underage, he said no, so they beat him up. When they drove off, they backed over him. Grissom explains that Brian was deaf, and had no idea what they were asking of him, and that's why he reacted the way he did. Mark requests an attorney.

At the coffee shop, they theorize that Kendall entered to kill Erin and then got excited and killed everyone else by mistake.

The episode ends with Grissom telling Dr. Gilbert that his mother was deaf, and taught him to sign.

Justice is Served

This is the twenty first episode of the first season of CSI Las Vegas.

Synopsis

The first shot is of a man running through a type of foliage more likely to be found in upstate New York than in Vegas. His jog is interrupted when he is attacked by an enormous cat.

Grissom and his team appear, making their way down through running trial which is as green as a golf course. An unnamed person runs through, glances at the fallen runner, and takes off into the verdant, lush, non-native greenery. Warrick surmises that the runner had been dragged down from the trail to be gutted. Closer examination, however, leads him to believe that the man was eviscerated not by a mountain lion, but by a scalpel.

Back a the office, Catherine and Grissom discuss the other body that turned up that night: a six-year-old girl died on a carnival ride a few blocks over, and she wants the case. Gil gives her the case but tells her to take Sara with her.

Gil then stops by the morgue where the coroner informs him that a scalpel-wielding mountain lion did not disembowel the jogger, it was a dog, which may or may not have been able to use a scalpel as well. If the dog couldn't manage a scalpel, it's possible that after the dog downed the jogger, an opportunistic creature with opposable thumbs appeared to harvest some internal organs.

Catherine and Sara make their way to the carnival and as they view the body of the six year old girl, they both seem to become personally involved with the case since they are both women and women are, of course, ruled by their maternal instincts and unable to function objectively. They interview the mother, who says that the girl was there one minute, and had fallen off the ride the next.

While Sara and Catherine weep at the carnival, interrogate carnies, and collect a urine sample from one of them, Nicky and Warrick collect dog feces and lice where the runner was killed.

The lab tech, from making a mold of the wound, has surmised that the dog has only forty two teeth and is a Great Dane/Mastiff mix. It is not long before they find the dog in question. They visit the home where the dog lives but it attacks Nick, and they quickly learn he's missing a tooth. The dog's mom is a physical therapist that works with athletes, one of which is Terry Manning – the dead runner. They take the dog into custody.

Back at CSI Central, Catherine learns that the carnie whose urine she collected was clean. She is floored until it is revealed that the lab tech made a mistake and switched his with a woman's. Or that the carnie had a stash of urine so he could be prepared in case he was asked for a drug test. Sara calls OSHA and learns that the carnival is wanted in eight states for assorted unspecified violations and staffed by many ex-felons, including the boss, Roger Pete, a convicted sex offender on parole.

Catherine returns to the carnie whose urine sample she took and we see him muttering that he "didn't know she was under eighteen" and comparing his love life with that of Jerry Lewis before he gets around to asking what this has to do with their investigation. They finally ask him to describe what happened: he saw the mother come running out of the tunnel screaming for her daughter. He and Joey, operator, hit the kill switch and stop the ride, ran into the tunnel to look for the little girl, but they found her face down in a pool of water. Catherine notes that this doesn't match with the mother's story.

At the lab, they are unable to confirm that the dog, Simba, killed the jogger. Warrick reveals that the ice he collected was actually dry ice, and explains that surgical teams use dry ice to pack organs shipped for transplant.

They return to Susan's place and take a sample of dog crap. Grissom looks in her fridge and notes that she has a system of labeled containers in it to keep the contents neatly organized, possibly because she works in sports nutrition and needs to keep everyone's diet straight. Grissom comments that she's not terribly upset about the fact that her pet might be put down but she goes into a tyrant about how everything eventually dies but if clients take her advice and eat properly they can cheat time. Susan then diagnoses Gil as being short on a supplement found in beets and whips him up a smoothie with beets in it.

Warrick interrupts to tell Grissom that he found an extremely well-maintained set of antique surgical tools, kept near the door. Just then, one of her clients arrives and she ushers him into her home office.

The little girl, meanwhile, has been processed and it's been determined that she drowned and had a fractured forearm. It was a spiral fracture because her arm was twisted, probably seconds before her death. As Catherine leaves the morgue, she runs into Sandy's mom, and Catherine asks her once again to describe what happened in detail. Her eyeballs are firmly in the left corners of her eyes while she tells the story. Catherine decides to take in the entire Tunnel Of Love ride as evidence.

Nicky enters the lab and tells Warrick that the fecal sample he took in Susan's backyard matches with one they found at the crime scene and has human tissue in it, and the human tissue matches the jogger's DNA. They check the surgical tools for blood: they have blood on them. But it's antique blood.

They have also taken a bunch of stuff from her kitchen, and spray luminol on all of it. Two items glow positive: the blender, and the drinking glass Susan was using earlier.

Catherine and Sara are trying to figure out what happened, using the ride and a few dummies. They conclude that the only person who could have done it was whoever sat next to her. Catherine bitterly says that the mom was looking left when she told her about the accident. When a person is remembering, they look right, and creating, they look left.

Grissom et al pay another visit to Susan to tell her that they found blood in the blender that matched the jogger. She explains she got porphyria, a genetic disease that she's treating by eating the blood-rich organs of healthy people. She has her dog kill people, harvests the organs, and dries them so they can be used as protein powder. She's taken into custody.

Over at Carla Dantini's house, Catherine and Sara pay a visit, armed with the warrant. They note that Carla's watch is broken from water exposure and the lining of her sneakers did not run; these two observations suggest that she did not leap into the water for Sandy, but rather drowned her. Catherine goes on a tirade about infanticide and leaves as Carla is being taken into custody.

And in the last scene, Catherine goes to a random house and makes out with its occupant—the toothy building inspector from a couple episodes back.

Memorable Quotes

Dr. Hillridge: You want an empirical experience? There's a fresh shake in my fridge.
Sargeant: Let's go. Officer? She is nuts, right?
Grissom: She's a cold blooded killer.

Catherine: So you did the tox screen on my carny?

Greg: Roger that. You know, I have seen guys drink, like, five gallons of water to try and dilute their urine. It's the old straight flush. But all bad boy Sanders has to do is just test their specific gravity and-- blammo! -- I can still catch their toxic butts.

Catherine: Mm-hmm. So?

Greg: So your guy didn't do that.

Catherine: Great. What did he do? Try and mask it?

Greg: No.

Catherine: Oh, come on. That creep tested clean?

Greg: Yeah. For someone who's on the pill.

Nick: Man, do you turn it on like this at your seminars?

Grissom: People actually pay to go to my seminars, Nick. We've I.D.'d the dog.

Nick: Well, if he's got bits of jogger hanging out of his mouth, cuff him.

Greg: You know, most dogs have 42 teeth but, as you've discovered, your Cujo only has 41. Woof-woof.

Grissom: Did you ever hear a dog say "woof-woof," Greg? I mean, what is the origin of that? And what do we sound like to them, I wonder.

Greg: I don't know. Probably blah, blah, blah.

Catherine: Oh, before you came to Nevada you should have looked up the law. Mandatory drug testing wherever there's been an accident. Pee now, and don't tell me you're shy. Stay on him.

Sara: Mandatory drug testing?

Catherine: Yeah, well, there should be.

Warrick: This sucks! But it's evidence, right?

Nick: No, hair and fiber is evidence, Warrick. This is combat duty.

Warrick: Mountain lions are brutal.

Grissom: And smart... this one evidently knows how to use a scalpel.

Grissom: What?

Nick: Well, it's just that most people don't admit to being wrong.

Grissom: I'm wrong all the time. That's how eventually I get to "right".

Catherine: What?

Sara: Well, this is fun.

Catherine: As opposed to...?

Sara: A more scientific approach.

Dr Hillridge (to Grissom): I guess one mans corpse is another mans candy. Care for a sip of folacin?

Evaluation Day

This is the 22nd episode of the first season of CSI Las Vegas.

Synopsis

The episode opens with taxpayer dollars being thrown in the toilet as several police helicopters hover over a car of skinny women with big breasts who are in a BMW in their underwear. The car, however, has a large bloodstain on the bumper.

Soon, Grissom and Brass arrive, and open the trunk of a car. It contains the cut off head of a brunette man who, we learn, was killed six to eight hours ago.

Later, Catherine pays a visit to Grissom in his office and he reminds them that it's evaluation day, hence the mountain of paperwork before him. He commences with the delegating of the cases: Gil and Catherine will be working the disembodied head case. Nicky and Sara get another homicide, roughly 40 miles outside Baker.

Grissom then kicks everyone out of his office and invites Nick to sit down for his evaluation. Grissom opens the eval by saying: "Repeat after me: silk, silk, silk." Nicky does. Gil then asks, "What do cows drink?" "Milk," Nicky says. Grissom then informs him that cows drink water, and he's not ready to work solo.

Dr. Robbins the coroner, meanwhile, is listening to rock music and dancing. The rock music, it turns out, was performed by the guy with no head, Victor DaSilva. The head has a nasty wound on the top of it, and there are deep wounds on his jaw, perhaps from bad aim. Grissom asks Catherine if a woman could have done it. She says she could of. The coroner Gil if he wants to find out exactly what tools were used to bludgeon Victor, they'll have to boil his head in laundry detergent.

Warrick meanwhile has run into the man whose grandson used his car to kill someone many episodes back. He's upset because there was a brawl at juvie and if his son squeals, his sentence will be reduced but he'll be killed by his peers. If he doesn't squeal, he'll get a longer sentence, The girls who were cruising around in their underwear are wrapped in police blankets and shivering in the tank as they look across the table Brass and Catherine, who want to know how a severed head got in their trunk. The blonde replies indignantly that they may have stolen the car, but they had no idea there was a head in the trunk. Her friend agrees. The blonde elaborates, saying they lost their friends at Bar 9-1-1 with no ride home, and started doing shots of tequila with some guy who looked like Cat Stevens in his van, and the had a ball, but then he said something creepy, which was: "I met this girl, on the Internet, who offered me a round-trip ticket to fly out there and end her life. She wanted me to shove a tennis ball down her throat."

They fly out of the van in their undies and the nearest is a luxury vehicle with the keys in the ignition and so they steal it. Brass then he books them on charges relating to the car theft and the drunken driving.

Back at CSI, James is explaining how life in Juvie works. He starts by explaining that "First off, this place only sees two colors, black and white. You stay with your own." The peer pressure to self-segregate by color is accelerated by the presence of a gang from Los Angeles. The straw came: Las Vegas gang member and an LA gang member had a disagreement while James happened to be in his bunk. One was killed by the other and James was the only witness.

Nick and Sara drive to the body that was found outside of Baker. It is covered with flies, and is missing the head, hands, feet and skin. There are no footprints around the body except for those of the police, and the body is lying in a crater. Sara looks at the sky, perhaps opining that it had fallen from a plane.

Warrick then goes to juvie and for some reason, is recognized by many inhabitants as CSI. The blood from the stabbed kid is still fresh on the floor and someone has stuffed a bloody t-shirt into a toilet. He fishes it out and underneath it is a knife.

Dr. Robbins, meanwhile, is standing over the body Nicky and Sara somehow managed to bring back to headquarters and learning about the oddities of its proportion: the shoulders are too wide in relation to the torso, and the leg bones are too thick. Dr. Robbins concludes that it can't be Victor DaSilva's body because the body is not of a human. He says he has no idea what it could be the body of, since he knows of no animal that is built so much like a human. Apparently Dr. Robbins made it through his entire education without ever learning about a certain order of animal called "primates", and went his whole life blissfully ignorant about the discovery channel.

Meanwhile, the lab tech found something stuck underneath the brake pedal of the BMW. After a lengthy and soporific lead up, he reveals he found peanuts. "It's one of those funny clues. Could be nothing, could mean everything," Sara muses. Nicky, still insecure because he told his boss that cows drink milk, can only think to say: "Hmmm."

At DaSilva's apartment, Grissom meets Trent, who is currently painting. The entire place is draped in plastic tarps and covered in fresh paint. Brass and Grissom poke around and they find a snapshot of Victor, with another person cut out of the picture. Grissom then checks the shoes of the victim for peanut shells, which he finds.

Teri Miller makes a guest appearance to help Dr. Robbins do his job, and teaches him about primates. She concludes that the body is a gorilla, and everyone stands in shocked silence.

Sara retreats to spend time in front of the computer, listening to a narrator talk about hunting gorillas for profit. Gil chides her: the gorilla isn't a person so it's not a murder and she shouldn't be wasting her time. She protests and Gil apologizes and explains that it was all part of her evaluation.

Meanwhile, Greg and Warrick are demonstrating how you can make a lethal weapon using only a toothbrush and a disposal razor blade. You melt the end of the toothbrush to insert the razor, then use a rubber band wrapped around the base to hide the blade.

Nicky and Catherine are investigating another murder at a storage facility and note bloody footprints in the hallway. The storage shed, it turns out, is rented out to Victor DaSilva. His body is there, without its head. They find two weapons: a hatchet with a blunt end counterbalancing the blade and a claw-headed hammer.

Moulds made of Victor's skull imply that he was hit in the head with the claw hammer, then struck with the ax. He was beheaded so he could fit in a small storage trunk.

Nicky, meanwhile, at DaSilva's apartment, explains to Sara his theory: the footprints at the crime scene were a size 11, the peanut shoes were a size 11, and DaSilva's a size 10. Nicky reaches in DaSilva's close: there is a peanut shell hiding in the cuff of a pair of khaki pants.. The are part of a jumpsuit uniform for Spur's Corral, a restaurant where you get peanuts on the tables.

Dr. Robbins, meanwhile, disagrees with everyone's theories about how DaSilva died. He says he was killed by a point-blank shot to the heart.

Later, Brass and Gil are standing in the lobby of Spur's Corral and eating peanuts as they wait for the host or hostess to seat them. Nicky is there too, trying to link the uniform he found in the closet with Victor DaSilva. Gil then notices that a sombrero hanging behind Nicky's head matches the one in the snapshot of DaSilva Brass found earlier. Gil looks carefully at the picture and notices that Victor left an ear in when he was cutting the person out. The ear had earrings, and a hostess identified the person the ear was attached to as Fred Applewhite.

Later, Nicky and Catherine coat Applewhite's feet with ink and order him to walk, and then run. Grissom explains how a walking footstep -- which shows the entire foot -- differs from the running footstep, which demonstrates only where the pressure was. After explaining at length footprints are as unique as snowflakes, they conclude that Applewhite's footprints put him at the scene of the crime.

Apparently Victor and Fred were partners until Victor dumped him for someone new. Fred and Vic got in a fight, Vic was killed Fred tried to stuff the body in a footlocker, and then cut his head off and ran car with the head. Fred went back to lock the shed, and in those few minutes, two girls in their underwear took his car.

Warrick talks Ronnie Conners about the stabbing. Ronnie's nickname, is macaroni, and he is very proud of this for some reason. The weapon he made will incriminate him, because he shaved with the razor before attaching it to the toothbrush.

The final shot is of Gil and Warrick enjoying a roller coaster ride.

Memorable Quotes

Nick: Peanuts? On the gas pedal?
Sara: It's one of those funny clues. Could mean nothing, could mean everything.

Grissom: Do you think a woman could've done this?
Catherine: I could.
Grissom: Scared of you.

Sara: I can't believe you. You, with your pet tarantula your maggot farms, that komodo dragon on back order...

Doc Robbins: Uh, voice sound familiar?
Catherine: Kind of sounds like the daytime coroner.
Grissom: Gary Telgenhoff?
Doc Robbins: Yep. A songwriter in his off-time. What do you think?

Catherine: It sucks.

Doc Robbins: Hmm.

Catherine: Hey, I just filed for divorce. I'm feeling a little confident.

Catherine: Okay, let's get right to it. What's your shoe size?

Trent Calloway: Why?

Catherine: I have a shoe fetish. I love feet.

Greg: Squirrels love 'em ... they get tossed at dodger stadium and they make a hell of a butter.

Sara: You're nuts. You know that.

Greg: Exactamundo. Peanuts!

Nick: Look, I'm not one of your suspects you can trick, okay? If I'm not ready, be a man.. tell me I'm not ready.

Grissom: You're not ready.

Nick: You know why I took this job? Honestly? I wanted to pack heat, walk under the yellow tape, be the man ... but mostly, because I want you to think I'm a good CSI.

Grissom: And that's the reason I have to hold you back. Anybody who's great at anything, Nick, does it for their own approval not someone else's.

Grissom: Mr. Callaway, is there a remote possibility that Victor DiSilva ever worked at a concession stand of some sort? Like at a ball park or...the secret garden of Siegfried and Roy, in the elephant's habitat?

Callaway: I don't think it's Victor's style. This is ridiculous.

Grissom: Repeat after me. Silk, silk, silk.

Nick: Silk, silk, silk.

Grissom: What do cows drink?

Nick: Milk.

Grissom: Cows drink water. They produce milk.

Later

Nick: Hey, Catherine, say, "Silk, silk, silk."

Catherine: Silk, silk, silk.

Nick: What do cows drink?

Catherine: Water. Why?

Nick: Never mind.

Sara: What has gotten in to you?

Nick: Grissom.

Prisoner : Hey, what you got in the tackle box, babe? You going fishing?

Catherine: Now there's a start, "gross." Gross negligence, flying down I-15 in a stolen car. Gross anatomy, a human bowling ball in the trunk. Gross details, let's hear it.

Brass : I don't think you two are murderers, I think you're just felony stupid.

Grissom: Someone lost their head and then... someone lost their head.

Warrick: Whatever happened to my evaluation?
Grissom: You're sittin in it.

The Strip Strangler

This is the 23rd and final episode of the first season of CSI Las Vegas.

Synopsis

It's a dark and stormy night in Las Vegas. The camera pans from an external shot of the Saturn Arms apartment complex to an interior shot of an apartment. We hear a popping noise, and a young woman sits up, but soon lies down, convinced she's only hearing things. Again she hears a noise, and again she is startled. This time, unfortunately, there's an intruder standing next to her bed.

Gil and Brass enter the bedroom. She has been left with her hands tied to her headboard. Her name is Eileen Jane Snow, discovered only after the woman with whom she carpooled in the morning couldn't get anyone to answer the door. We learn that she is the third body to turn up lately that shows signs of being the victim of a serial killer. The killer has done the same to all victims: he administers three or four overpowering blows to the head with a homemade weapon made at the scene, forces them to drink sodium pentathol, rapes her with an object, strangles, ejaculates on the bedsheets; then poses her as a pin-up."

Sara arrives soon, and predictably is upset. Gil firmly tells her to abandon her emotions and be impartial. . Sara searches the scene notes that she hasn't found one. The vacuum cleaner bag has been taken. Gil dispatches Catherine to check on all sex offenders and peeping Toms within a two mile radius. Suddenly Warrick tells them not to move—he found a hair.

Gil's walking toward the growing crowd surrounding the house with Sheriff Mobley, and both are upset because the FBI is now involved. We soon meet Special Agent Culpepper, FBI, who informs him that the investigation will run through him. They agree, tersely, to work together on it.

Gil crosses to the tape line to talk to Syd Goggle, a security guard, who has little helpful insights to give, and exasperated, Grissom storms back to where he came from. Later, Nick and Grissom visit the coroner. CSI then provides a flashback sequence as to how the woman suffered, allowing the audience to witness her getting smacked around and abused and further glamorizing misogyny. Apparently, the sodium pentathol allowed him to torture her for six hours. He choked her unconscious and brought her to multiple times, and was raped by objects. (THIS IS ON PRIMETIME TV. We can't see Janet Jackson willingly show us her left tit but we can watch a play by play of a woman being brutally raped and tortured? Which we are only watching because the victim is hot? Mark my words—we will never see, say, an overweight woman in her mid forties being raped in a vivid flashback. Only hot chicks.) . There is also an "everyday polymer" embedded in her uterine wall. Dr. Robbins adds that he found something missing on the previous two victims: two fibers, one in the back of Eileen's throat, one stuck between two of her teeth. The fiber is white cotton, possibly from a towel. Meanwhile, Greg is telling Catherine that the semen he found on the sheets matches the semen taken from the other scenes but there's a red substance mixed in.

Sara has been hard at work as well: she's matched the hair Warrick found to the hair found on a previous crime scene, but there's no way they can make a DNA match, since there's no skin tag attached to the hair. They wonder if the killer planted it.

In the hall, Nick runs into Grissom and tells him that he got a page about a meeting on the case. Grissom is unaware of such a meeting. Gil crashes the meeting anyway, and Culpepper sidesteps his accusation of dis-inviting him on purpose. Grissom orders his crew to get out and go back to his office. He Gil then turns back to Culpepper and says, "I'll be happy to pass back any pertinent information you may have to my team." Apparently, unbeknownst to Grissom, Sara has volunteered to work with the FBI as a decoy for an operation wherein the Feds plan to set up and entrap the serial killer. Apparently she matches the victim prototype to a T: she's hot, and in TVland, serial killers only go after good looking, white, skinny women in their late 20s or early thirties. In the real world this isn't true. If you don't believe me, look up the BTK victims. Anyway Grissom is against it but Culpepper asks him to come up with something better, he doesn't want to put his CSI in danger. Sara, however, interrupts to assure him she's interested in risking rape and murder.

Nick goes back to Elaine's apartment and combs it for evidence. He finds a scrap of a latex glove. The viewer gets a flashback of the killer in gloves. As he thinks about this, he realizes there is a reporter hiding in the closet. She asserts that The Public has a Right To Know even if it means she contaminates the crime scene. He kicks her out.

The lab tech, meanwhile, has figured out what the red stuff is in the semen: It's C_{12}, H_{22}, O_{11}, NaCl, H_2O, and tomato paste. Or in English: sugar, salt, water, and ketchup.

Apparently the killer adds it afterwards, perhaps to mask his DNA.

She goes to Grissom's office. He's caught on to the fact that she's cooperating with the FBI and she's being groomed to take his place. So they stare each other down. Nick interrupts to tell them that he discovered that the killer wears latex gloves, and they wonder aloud if it could be Paul Millander striking again.

Soon, we find ourselves at the market where the killer allegedly selects his victims. Sara has dressed for the occasion, slathering on Wet N Wild and wearing a top that was perhaps selected from a children's store. Grissom tells her that they are better off looking at the killer's past actions to dictate his future ones; this is action for the sake of action. He doesn't convince anyone. If he did, after all, Sara wouldn't have to trollop up anymore and the ratings might suffer from the lack of T and A.

She wanders around the store for three hours and nothing happens. They wonder if they should reposition her at a Borders (shameless plug. Product placement.) Meanwhile, as Sara pretends to be doing something in the grocery store besides aimlessly wandering, a scruffy looking guy tries to steal from her purse. He is swarmed by Feds. This effectively ruins the sting for the future since the guy will know the Feds are watching him.

Over at the Hotel Monaco, they reconvene to study the latest victim. This one is married. Her husband was playing downstairs, and when he came up, she was dead. She had been strangled with the cord of a lamp. The killer didn't ejaculate on the sheets this time but they still think it's the same guy: chemical restraint, death by strangulation. This time, no object rape: they found a scrap of cross-hatched leather with tiny air holes.

Meanwhile, Culpepper is questioning the victim's husband, noting they spent the weekend apart even though they paid money to check into a hotel in their hometown. He liked gambling and she liked to read so it was the "perfect getaway". During the questioning, Grissom strides in. He asks if he can see the man's golf clubs, wanting to know if the leather on the club handles matches the leather on the object used on his wife. The golf bag is locked and is always kept locked—making it unlikely that someone else stole the golf club handle to do it. Gil finds the club that matches the missing scrap and hands it over to Culpepper. The man is arrested for the four murders. Gil, however, says that the man wasn't guilty of the previous three murders. He insists the man read the papers and copied the real killer.

Culpepper, disagreeing for no real reason, pulls rank, insisting that the married woman fits the single-woman victim type to a T.

Later we learn that Walden was having an affair. At a press conference where Culpepper is telling everyone he caught the killer, Grissom says, "I'm telling you, this guy did not kill those other women." The reporter that was at the scene with Nicky turns to question him further but he clams up.

The Sheriff proceeds to upbraid Grissom, and tells him to take two weeks off. He packs up his stuff and tells his staff that Catherine is in charge.

He goes home but Catherine drops by unannounced to tell him she declined the offer to become the boss. She wants the promotion on merit, not because Grissom is a disaster at PR. The CSIs, apparently, feel the same way and are waiting outside. They come in and they begin to discuss the case. He tells them take the victims one by one and go over everything with a fine toothed comb.

Meanwhile Catherine is trying to match the semen with that of convicted sex offenders. She matches it to one Hunter S. Baumgartner, arrested and released for indecent exposure.

Next Grissom and Catherine are entering the dive bar where Baumgartner works. They get down to business. He recognizes the victims from TV, he says, but that's all. They ask him why the semen was on the sheets and he shrugs and tells them he's gay and a prostitute for men; the only reason why he'd be in a woman's bedroom is to help her with interior décor. . Catherine asks whether any recent tricks asked for a "portable" sample of Baumgartner's DNA. He says yes but there were too many to count. He wanders off and they realize the serial killer is planting semen.

Back at the C.S.I. Château, Sara's telling Gil that she hasn't been able to find anything new with regard to Tracy Berg. However, Warrick went back to Audrey Hayes's apartment and found white cotton fibers around the point of entry. They wonder if the fibers. All three women went to Strong's Gym once in the last three months. Warrick decides to go to the gym and get sample towels and Sara, meanwhile, will be looking over a list of the club's male gym members. The two troop off to begin their work as Gil's phone rings.

Later, we learn that Syd Goggle's claim that someone peeled out of Elaine's driveway is false. Nick is on the phone with Grissom about this information and has to get off quickly when Culpepper comes in. On his end, Gil's flashing back to Syd Goggle's initial offer to help.

He goes to Goggle's apartment, and when discovering he's not home, breaks in and enters without a warrant. As Gil looks around, he notices a tray filled with shaving gear, and instantly flashes to Syd sitting in front of the television and shaving himself. He opens the kitchen trash bags, noting the ketchup packets scattered about, and then moves on to the basement washing mashing. Oops. Syd is there. Syd tells him that he's laundering some gym towels, and when Gil smirks, pleased with himself, Syd takes off his wig. He asks Goggle if the women rejected him at Strong's Gym so he stuffed the club's towels down their throats to retaliate.

Goggle says they can't trace towels. Gil begs to differ, and taunts him about getting caught. Goggle hits him in the head with a wrench. Gil goes and Goggle's about to follow his initial blow with a sledgehammer, but is stopped by the half-dozen bullets that appear out of nowhere and land in his chest. It was Catherine. She comes down to check on Gil, and Culpepper's behind her. Everyone stands around and looks at the body. Gil numbly says, "I just wanted to talk to him."

They have another press conference, the fact that Gil was breaking and entering with no warrant when suspended, no less, is not mentioned, Culpepper gets all the credit, and everything goes back to normal.

Memorable Quotes

Grissom: The last time a security guard tried to help me, he ended up dead.

Greg: Freaky, huh?
Catherine: Freakiest sperm I've seen in a while.

Greg: You got a hot dog?
Catherine: This one of your jokes, Greg?
Greg: I got the ketchup.
Catherine: I'm sure this is meaningful.
Greg: I went back and looked at the ejaculate from the last two murders. The same thing. "Indeterminate red stuff." It's c12, h22 and o11, nacl, h2o and tomato paste.
Catherine: Sugar, water, salt and tomato paste. Ketchup?
Greg: Ketchup.

Grissom: Did you come here to tell me about your new job?
Catherine: I told the Sheriff I'd pass.
Grissom: You don't want to be a supervisor?

Catherine: Well, if I get a promotion, I want it to be on merit ... not because you're politically tone-deaf. So, our guys are outside in their Tahoes. If you're a civilian, we are. Except we are putting in for overtime.

Sara: He's escalating.

Grissom: That's the pattern. It's a continuum.

Sara: Guess he wants to get caught.

Grissom: Signature killers never want to get caught, and they won't stop until they do.

Lynda Darby: I'm sorry that I scared you.

Nick: You didn't scare me!

Lynda Darby: You wanna tell me what you found over by the window?

Nick: Nope.

Grissom: Sometimes, the hardest thing to do is to do nothing.

Grissom: Ah. Now that the trees are gone, I can almost see the forest.

Agent Culpepper: We'll work the "Strip Strangler" case in conjunction.

Grissom: The what?

Agent Culpepper: He strangles them near Las Vegas Boulevard then removes their clothes. Strip Strangler. Why? What do you call him?

Grissom: Unknown Signature Homicide, Metropolitan Las Vegas.

Agent Culpepper: Oh. He's not kidding, is he?

Catherine: When we zig, he zags.

Catherine: Never doubt. Never look back. That's how I live my life.

Grissom: I admire that.

Sara: Do we have a breakfast budget, Grissom?

Grissom: I believe Catherine was going to requisition one.

Sara: Good, cause our plates are up, and nobody has any money.

INDEX